\* \* \* \* \*

'This is written with so much heart. It's full of love and hope and liberation. Even the tougher stories are told with strength and the potential for change. From Stonewall to Jamaica to Canal Street, the writers speak with such honestly and insight, it's thrilling. And they're hilarious too! This book is so vital, it'll be a talisman for so many, a beacon, a path out of the shadows. It should be in every school and home, to reach out to those in need, or those remembering their own journey. It made me cry, it made me hoot, it made me rage and it made me think. I think, really, I learnt from this. The book contains so many voices from the next wave of queer identity, it taught me better ways to talk and react and help. That's wonderful!'
**– Russell T Davies, writer and producer of Queer as Folk**

\* \* \* \* \*

'None of us are born with prejudice, sadly it's something that is learned – with more books like this usualizing queer people there is hope for a future of inclusion and social justice where we simply become part of the fabric of our communities and coming out becomes a thing of the past.'
**– Dr Elly Barnes MBE, CEO and Founder of Educate & Celebrate**

\* \* \* \* \*

'These 27 inspirational personal stories reveal the breadth and diversity of coming out experiences from people of different ages, eras and cultural backgrounds, including both their triumphs and tribulations. But the common thread is courage, honesty, self-acceptance and dignity. This book is a must-read for LGBT+ teens and their families and teachers.'
**– Peter Tatchell, human rights campaigner**

\* \* \* \* \*

\* \* \* \* \*

'For many in our communities, coming out is a transformative and liberating experience, but one that can only be truly enjoyed when the world around them embraces them. From chosen family to friendships forged in solidarity, these coming out stories offer real-life insight and wisdom to those who've yet to take that next step in sharing themselves with the world. These stories are also a brilliant resource for parents and families who underestimate the power of acceptance and love to counter a world that can often be so cruel. Enjoy these stories, share these stories and revel in the vulnerability and honesty assembled here.'

*– Phyll Opoku-Gyimah aka Lady Phyll, Co-Founder and Executive Director of UK Black Pride*

\* \* \* \* \*

'Coming out is something that most LGBTQ+ people face at some point in their lives, whether it be a small, personal experience, or in a larger context. While every story is different, there are common threads to be found – the fear of rejection or violence, the knowledge that life after coming out is an undiscovered country but also, in many cases, the liberation and life-affirming experience that it often creates. This new book is a collection of stories about the process of coming out from a diverse selection of LGBTQ+ people. They are, in turn, funny, heartbreaking and empowering. A spotlight shone upon a pivotal moment in the lives of those within the LGBTQ+ community, from all backgrounds. Each is a mini biography, full of those nervous first steps and the hopes and fears of the person involved, with which many of us, having gone through similar experiences, can readily identify. It's also a history lesson in many ways; describing things that happened in the past which today would seem extreme. Yes, progress continues to be made, but as the more recent stories reveal, there's still a long way to go. I'm sure this book will be an inspiration to those still in the proverbial closet to perhaps take a leap into the wider world, one which waits to welcome them with open arms and open hearts.'

*– Annie Wallace, actress*

\* \* \* \* \*

\* \* \* \* \*

'This book is something I could have done with a long time ago. As it says so eloquently, we all just want to be loved by those we love for exactly who we are. But in 2020, homophobia is still rife and we still need to stand up and come out, which can be a daunting experience! This book is something I would have liked to give 16-year-old me as I was figuring out who I was! It shows that you're not alone and that every story is different and there is no right or wrong way to come out. I loved it.'

**– Stephen Bailey, comedian and presenter**

\* \* \* \* \*

'Coming out can be the most terrifying yet liberating moments in a queer person's life. This book perfectly captures the highs and lows of this life-changing process. Reading the authentic and vulnerable stories of people across the LGBTQ+ spectrum in this book reminds us that our struggle towards ultimate freedom is a collective one. Our stories are as diverse and unique as our community, but one thing is true in all of them – the powerful desire to overcome one's shame in the pursuit of a life worth living. This is a must-read for anyone grappling with the concept of coming out, and for those close to a queer person who want to understand what that journey must feel like.'

**– Riyadh Khalaf, broadcaster**

\* \* \* \* \*

'Uplifting and triumphant, each story is a feat of bravery and courage.'
**– Juno Dawson, author of This Book is Gay and What's the T?**

\* \* \* \* \*

'The stories here are rich and vivid – there is much for all of us to learn from this book.'
**– Joe Lycett, comedian and television presenter**

\* \* \* \* \*

# COMING OUT
# STORIES

*of related interest*

**Trans Teen Survival Guide**
*Owl Fisher and Fox Fisher*
ISBN 978 1 78592 341 8
eISBN 978 1 78450 662 9

**To My Trans Sisters**
*Edited by Charlie Craggs*
ISBN 978 1 78592 343 2
eISBN 978 1 78450 668 1

**How to Understand Your Gender**
*A Practical Guide for Exploring Who You Are*
*Alex Iantaffi and Meg-John Barker*
Foreword by S. Bear Bergman
ISBN 978 1 78592 746 1
eISBN 978 1 78450 517 2

**Trans Love**
*An Anthology of Transgender and Non-Binary Voices*
*Edited by Freiya Benson*
ISBN 978 1 78592 432 3
eISBN 978 1 78450 804 3

# COMING OUT STORIES

Personal Experiences of Coming Out from
Across the LGBTQ+ Spectrum

*Edited by Emma Goswell and Sam Walker*
*Foreword by Tim Sigsworth MBE*

**Jessica Kingsley Publishers**
London and Philadelphia

First published in Great Britain in 2021 by Jessica Kingsley Publishers
An Hachette Company

1

Copyright © Jessica Kingsley Publishers 2021
Foreword copyright © Tim Sigsworth 2021

Trigger Warning: This book mentions abuse, bullying, conversion therapy and depression.

A CIP catalogue record for this title is available from the British Library and the Library of Congress

ISBN 978 1 78775 495 9
eISBN 978 1 78775 496 6

Printed and bound in Great Britain by Clays Ltd

Jessica Kingsley Publishers' policy is to use papers that are natural, renewable and recyclable products and made from wood grown in sustainable forests. The logging and manufacturing processes are expected to conform to the environmental regulations of the country of origin.

Jessica Kingsley Publishers
Carmelite House
50 Victoria Embankment
London EC4Y 0DZ

www.jkp.com

**This book is dedicated to Abigail Goswell 28.06.73–15.10.20**

Thank you for being the best sister a girl could wish for. You may have disapproved of my hairstyles over the years, but you never judged me for being me! Thank you for inspiring me every single day. Love you to the moon and back.

And to my parents. Thanks for being incredible role models and teaching me how to be kind, how to love and how to throw a damn good party!

Emma

For the loves of my life, Lyla and Britta, may you grow up in a world where you are never afraid to be your wonderful selves.

Sam

# Contents

# Foreword

As someone who has worked and volunteered within the LGBTQ+ community for over 30 years, I have had the privilege of hearing people coming out to me throughout my adult life. Those stories have stayed with me and inspire me when I support others on the journey to coming out to their family, friends and others.

This book is an absolute joy, for whilst every story is different and people share both good and bad experiences of coming out, what every story does include is that first step on the journey – 'self-acceptance'. This pride in who you are is essential because, as so many people have said before, if you can't love yourself, how is someone else going to love you? Getting over our own inability to accept ourselves or any feelings of shame, as Kate retells in her story, is often the first step. These stories will, I hope, inspire many more LGBTQ+ people to find and accept themselves, to realize that they are not alone, that others have walked this well-worn path and, as I can confirm, that things do get better when we can be open and honest with ourselves and others about who we really are.

Emma Goswell and Sam Walker have spent their professional lives within the media being strong and passionate voices for the LGBTQ+ community, and I am proud to call them activists. They have both been a personal inspiration to me and to many others, and that is why this book is such a strong and important message to anyone who is thinking about coming out and/or feels alone and isolated, as well as being a call to action to allies who can provide support on the journey.

This book is not the painful retelling of the stories of victims. As Bill's story shows, even 47 years ago in a more challenging world for the LGBTQ+ community, some people did come out and receive love and support. We see amongst these pages 27 people who were, and are, incredibly brave and proud advocates who are living their lives fully. There is so much love, hope and humour in this book. It reflects not only the character of each writer but also the character of our community, which absolutely owns the trademarks to camp, the rainbow and a joy for living.

We are not told the current age of most of the people featured here. This for me captures the timelessness of these stories. They echo the stories I heard as a young man in the mid-1980s and I still recognize the words in the young people who come through our door at the national LGBTQ+ youth homelessness charity 'akt' (Albert Kennedy Trust), where we support young people who are seeking a safe place to stay after suffering rejection and often abuse from their families after coming out to them. The fact that, for some, coming out remains a difficult and painful process highlights the real need today for books like this which give hope, support and guidance.

This selection of stories acknowledges that no two journeys to accepting and being who we are will ever be the same. However, they all show that the challenges are outweighed by the hope for, and the reality of, a better future.

These 27 people have freely given a very personal insight into their lives. Therefore, I believe I should say something about my story. As a teenager I helped care for my father in his last years of life, whilst having a very difficult relationship with my mum. My much older siblings had left home already and I remained at home with my parents. My mum behind closed doors was mentally cruel to me both before, and especially after, I came out. At 15 I was so unhappy that I wanted to take my own life. I am so thankful to the person who helped me accept and love who I was at that point and stop myself. I kept this and my mum's behaviours hidden from my friends who came to visit, and when my dad died, I took the opportunity to go to university and leave that family life behind me.

Every coming out story is unique, and these stories show that clearly. However, they do contain some key elements. For example, Carl's story recognizes the double life we often lead before coming out and the pain that causes us and sometimes others in our life. His story also captures the amazing new journey we can open ourselves up to once we find the love and support to come out.

Ultimately, people must come out when they are ready. Whilst many people in this book were in their teens and twenties, some, like Kerry, realized later in life who they were. Others chose to wait until their personal circumstances had changed. I remember one man who waited until he was 60, by which time his mother had passed away.

Many people have to find the best moment when they feel safe to come out and be themselves; in some cases, this can be during the most bizarre situations. I remember one person telling me they came out to their dad whilst they were both paintballing, as they figured that he was having too much fun and was too preoccupied to react badly. There are so many ways to come out as these people's stories show, from email, phone and in person – there's no right way other than feeling safe with your choice.

It is so important, as our community recognizes how beautifully diverse it is, that this book has captured people who identify across the intersections of gender, race, sexuality, faith, age and disability. Many people who come out face a more complex journey – for example, Enoch, GJ and Asad describe in their stories how they faced not only the potential of rejection by their family but also the loss of the wider cultural or faith community they were part of. This can include people being faced with painful choices between remaining part of a religious household or being who they are. Whilst many parents find ways to make adjustments in their approach to their faith in order to keep their love for their child strong, where this does not occur an LGBTQ+ person can find that their whole support system, which is wrapped up in their faith and community, has been lost when they come out.

Love it or hate it, some of the people in this book found their acceptance, friends and even safe home amongst the LGBTQ+ bars, clubs and cafés within their local gay scene. Indeed, for some of the storytellers in this book who came out pre-internet, this was a crucial lifeline in becoming their true selves.

I would recommend this book not just to LGBTQ+ people but to their parents in particular, as these stories give people a privileged insight into the worlds of 27 incredible LGBTQ+ people. I remember one mother I comforted who found out her son was gay in the most tragic way – through his suicide note. He wrote: 'I didn't want to bring shame and disappointment into your life by telling you who I am. I love you, Mum.' She said she had always known he was gay but just didn't know how to bring it up in conversation. For those parents who pick up this book, I hope you find the words amongst these incredible people's stories to have that first conversation with your child. There are also, of course, organizations like FFLAG[1] out there, run by other parents who can help you find the words you need to talk with and support your child as they come out.

We never stop coming out to people in our lives, and this book is a reminder that sometimes it can be a joyous thing, a realization of just how much those around us love and understand us. However, for some of us, it can be a painful realization that, whilst we have the acceptance of many, we still have a long way to go in securing the respect and equity which is our right in society.

Many of us first come out to a straight ally rather than another LGBTQ+ person. Allies can be truly inspirational, as Christine's story proved, when her parents demonstrated their continued love and support for her when she told them of her trans identity in the 1970s. It's easy to think that the majority are still against us, but this is not always the case. In fact, it's important that in fighting for our rightful place in society we remember that allies can be perfectly placed to exert a level of understanding and awareness outside our community that we could never achieve on our own.

Unlike Martin in his story, I feel fortunate to have come out post the Sexual Offences Act 1967, even thought I was still labelled a criminal and 'mentally unwell' for being an out gay man at the age of 16 in 1984. This book is littered with people just like me who became activists within the LGBTQ+ community in response to their rejection both by those they loved and by an unaccepting society.

However well or badly our coming out goes within our

---

1    FFLAG (Families and Friends of Lesbians and Gays) is a charity supporting parents and their lesbian, gay, bisexual and trans sons and daughters. For further details, please visit www.fflag.org.uk

families, we are faced today with a world which has progressed, but still, in many countries, we are denied our civil and human rights. Trans people are facing the most aggressive challenges to their basic and legal right to equality and equity in society right now. This is why coming out and telling our stories is still so important in creating a visible community who are strong enough to challenge the apathy towards, and in some cases reversal of, our hard-won rights.

When you read these stories, you will see how for so many people campaigning together has been, and still is, part of our journey to self-empowerment, self-acceptance and key to forming our wonderful, logical queer families who help us to fully enjoy our queer lives through their love, humour and support.

As I write this piece in 2020, during a time when the world is facing the COVID-19 crisis, I am reminded of those people who came out during the last pandemic which devasted the LGBTQ+ community in particular. As someone who came out during the height of the AIDS crisis, I know the challenges and feeling of absolute fear that it presented. My mother reacted badly, informing me I was disgusting and would die alone of AIDS. I never told my friends what I was going through at home, for fear of losing them. I can confirm from my own charity that young people during this current pandemic are living in fear, and some are facing hostility and abuse from their families as they find themselves trapped at home in isolation during lockdown. However, as I discovered, the world as an out person post pandemic can be, and is, filled with opportunities and love.

My advice to anyone who is considering coming out to someone is to take your time; only you will know when you are ready to take this step. When you *are* ready, seek out support from an organization or person who has been there before you; and choose the person you come out to carefully – you should feel safe around them and feel confident that they are the kind of person who will give you the support you need when telling others. For me that was my last girlfriend, Erica, who when we were both 15 helped me love myself rather than fall in love with her! I personally think Erica had a lucky escape – well, at least according to my partner!

This book doesn't promise, or guide you to, a perfect future, but instead inspires hope; and I only wish I had been able to read these stories in 1983 as a petrified young man who wanted to tell the world who I really was.

Finally, please remember there is always room for love, and you will find support, inspiration, respect and love from people who you never thought would be there for you, even if others you thought would be there may disappoint you at first. I know that after coming out you will find your own logical queer family, a group of friends who will be with you when you need them most.

*Tim Sigsworth MBE, Chief Executive at akt*
*Out and proud for 37 years*

# Coming Out
## Emma's Introduction

Coming Out. What a load of drama! Who wants to talk about who they're having sex with – or even want to have sex with – with their nearest and dearest, and especially parents? Not me!

It's really nobody's business who you want to get naked with or which gender you identify as. But the truth is, we all want to be loved and accepted by our friends and family for who we are. We don't want to lie; we want to be us. We want those we care about to share the highs and lows of our life. The good dates, the bad dates, the heartthrobs and the heartbreaks. And that means being honest. About everything.

So, if you're LGBTQ+, it's likely you're going to have to come out at some point, which means you're probably going to have to have the 'coming out conversation'.

Yes, I'd love us to be living in utopia where labels don't matter and sexuality and gender are irrelevant. I'd love us to be at the point where coming out is a redundant non-event. Straight, cis-gendered people don't have to come out and I'd love us to live in a world where we don't have to either. I'd love straight people and LGBTQ+ people to get on with their lives and live in harmony without judgement. We're not there yet though, are we?

Sadly, as I write this in 2020, homophobia and transphobia are rife. Even in 2017, research published by Stonewall showed that one in five LGBT people had experienced a hate crime in the last 12 months because of their sexuality or gender identity. That rose to two in five for trans people![1]

And the picture isn't getting any better. According to Home Office figures in 2019, all hate crimes had increased by 10 per cent since the previous year, but for crimes based on sexuality it was a 25 per cent increase.[2] The Home Office say that's partly due to improvements in police recording, but it's still hugely worrying. The last thing I want to do is scare people. But honestly, coming out is not without its risks.

Admitting you're gay or trans or non-binary is still a conversation and a process that can bring the most confident soul, surrounded by liberal thinkers, out in a cold sweat. Years of hearing nonsense like 'It's Adam and Eve, not Adam and Steve', 'Don't be such a girl' or 'It's not normal' takes its toll on all of us. As one person I spoke to brilliantly put it: 'I was raised by straight people and I was being taught to live in their world.' He, like many people, simply learnt to fit in. And hide.

But hiding only gets you so far in life. Whether you get to 18 (as I was) or 78, most of us get to the stage where hiding becomes too much of a burden and only by coming out can we truly be ourselves and truly be happy. This book is essentially about that journey to happiness and acceptance.

As a broadcaster and podcaster, I've been lucky enough to speak to hundreds of people from across the UK and the USA

---

1   Stonewall (2017). *LGBT in Britain – Hate Crime and Discrimination: Based on You-Gov polling of more than 5000 LGBT people in Britain.* Retrieved from www.stonewall. org.uk/lgbt-britain-hate-crime-and-discrimination on 12 May 2020.

2   Home Office (2019). *Hate Crime, England and Wales, 2018/19.* Retrieved from https://assets.publishing.service.gov.uk/government/uploads/system/uploads/ attachment_data/file/839172/hate-crime-1819-hosb2419.pdf on 12 May 2020.

to hear their stories about coming out as lesbian, gay, bisexual, queer, trans, gender fluid or non-binary.

Everyone I've spoken to has been met with acceptance and love. Eventually.

That's not to say that some LGBTQ+ people still face losing people close to them, and even their home. I've spoken to people who have never spoken to their parents since they came out. I've spoken to people who have experienced bullying, violence, homelessness and severe isolation. I've even spoken to someone who has been through so-called 'conversion therapy', another who was threatened with a lobotomy and someone who was blackmailed because of their sexuality. Some have had it incredibly tough.

I spoke to one lesbian whose dad poured her a beer to celebrate when she came out, but few parents throw a big old party when their child announces they're gay or trans. Most take time to process it. Sometimes that takes days, weeks or months. Sometimes it takes years. But even the most reactionary parents tend to come around in the end. I've spoken to dozens of people who have been disappointed or angry with their parents' reaction. But I also spoke to someone who made a very good point: 'You may have spent months or years coming to terms with and understanding your own sexuality or gender identity, but it *may* be the first time your parents ever considered that you might be part of the rainbow family. Sometimes the first thing that comes out of their mouth isn't the ideal response, but remember it isn't their final response.' I spoke to another lesbian whose mum didn't speak to her for a few days and was so upset she threatened to divorce her dad. Fast forward six months and she accompanied her daughter out to gay bars and met her girlfriend. A few months after that she sent her daughter a birthday card with a rainbow on it and told her she'd chosen it because it looked like a pride rainbow.

Yes, there are horror stories in this book – moments that will reduce you to tears – but I think that last story sums up the one common thread in all the stories we've collected. And that is, it does get better!

Even for the very few who never speak to their family again there is another type of reconciliation or kind of happy ending: a realization that life does go on and that family doesn't have to mean blood. I've spoken to plenty of LGBTQ+ people who have found their own rainbow family made up of partners and friends. Out gay writer Armistead Maupin even has a phrase for it. He says he values his 'logical family' over his biological family.

The thing about coming out is that every story is as individual as the person telling it. Whether it's a celebrity, someone with an MBE, a teenager, or an older person who hasn't been able to talk about their sexuality their whole life, each story is beautifully unique. Within this book you'll hear from people who sat their family down for the 'chat', others who called their parents on the phone, some who wrote letters or emails and one who came out on stage! You'll also hear from people who went through long periods of confusion – only to be told *by their parents* (usually their mother) that they were gay!

Sometimes the moments are dramatic and heartfelt, filled with pathos, angst, uncertainty, tears and declarations of love. Other times they're spectacularly banal! I remember speaking to one gay man who simply went home and said, 'Mum, Dad, this is my boyfriend. Can you talk to him while I go upstairs to get changed? Then we're going out shopping!' No drama. Obviously, the guy concerned was pretty confident his parents weren't going to disown him or cause a scene, but I do think it's a good reminder that coming out can be done in very subtle, small ways. When you've done it a few times, it certainly becomes less stressful and something you could slip into conversation without it having to be a big deal. Office small talk with a new colleague could easily result in a small 'outing'. 'How was my weekend? Oh great, my boyfriend and I went to the cinema...' No big deal, but you've let someone know how you identify, as well as what a great weekend you've had. If you're LGBTQ+, you'll find yourself coming out continually and it honestly does get easier every time.

You'll also realize through reading this book that coming out is an evolving process. Identities can change. Just because you come out as one thing tomorrow doesn't mean that you might not come out as something else a few years down the line. I've heard from: trans men who have come out first as lesbians; from women who have come out as trans and then as bisexual; from men who have come out as gay and then gender fluid; from women who have come out as pansexual and then as polyamorous; from men who have come out as bisexual and then as non-binary. The list is endless and as diverse as the rainbow family that created it.

One thing that's pretty universal is that people who have come out say they almost *had* to for peace of mind. LGBTQ+ shame is a very real thing. Living a lie is something that cuts people up inside and has a massively detrimental effect on wellbeing. For many LGBTQ+ people, coming out has involved a huge struggle with their mental health. For some there's been a real struggle with drug or alcohol addiction too. I think everyone I've spoken to agrees that they're happier having come out and come through the other side. I know I am. I can remember, like it was yesterday, being 17 and thinking I was the only lesbian in the world and my secret was so awful that I couldn't tell anyone. I remember feeling sick with anxiety and having a deep sense of shame about who I was. It was a horrible place to be and the thought of coming out was terrifying. I'm beyond glad

I did though. Being gay is just a small part of my identity but something I'm now immensely proud of. It took time to learn to be happy and out and proud, but I got there.

We didn't start the podcast or compile this book to encourage you to come out. Far from it. Deciding to come out is an intensely personal thing; and if you are LGBTQ+, you should never be forced to do it before you're ready. Only you will know when the time is right.

We really started the podcast so that those who were thinking of coming out had a resource to go to. Somewhere to hear inspirational stories about how it had panned out for others in our rainbow family.

We also wanted to give some insight to parents, family members or friends who have LGBTQ+ people in their life but don't really understand their journey or their experience. So many people I've spoken to have parents who still think that being gay or trans or non-binary is a choice or a phase. I really wanted to give people some understanding of the inner turmoil and confusion that many of us go through before deciding to come out. You'll find within this book some examples of terrible parenting (those who have never spoken to their child again), some award-winning parents who have shown great understanding and kindness, and every type of parent or carer in-between.

Whoever you are, I hope in these pages you find a story that resonates and that you can identify with. A story that will inspire you and give you courage and hope for the future. And however you identify, if you are thinking of coming out, can I be the first to say, 'Welcome to the family!'?

# Come Out for LGBTQ+
## Sam's Introduction

My best friend came out to me when we were 16. Like so many best friends in this book, I already presumed he was gay. It wasn't that I was annoyed he hadn't said anything to me already, or I was desperate for him to say it. I had just realized it one day (I can't even remember when) and didn't care, so didn't think about it. I didn't grasp that he was burning up inside with fear that friends would reject him because of who he was. I'm still sorry he felt so desperately worried for so long.

As a straight, cis person, I've never had to come out. I've never had to uncomfortably correct the pronoun of my partner, answer an awkward question about a 'friend' or panic that I look so different in childhood photographs. I wonder how many straight, cis people even recognize this privilege?

However, I've had a lot of people come out to me – friends, relatives, colleagues, managers – and I've always thought how bloody annoying that must be. How many times must you have to do it? Do you feel nervous each time? Do you get fed up?

When my cousin told me that she had been secretly living with her lover for six months, I asked her how on earth she had kept it from her mum, who lived around the corner. 'Didn't she see the boxer shorts on the floor and the aftershave in the bathroom?' I asked. 'No,' she replied, 'because she's a girl.' I felt a bit daft that I'd presumed she was straight but I was excited and happy for her. When my aunt found out, she was not. When I asked how she could be upset that her daughter was in love and contented, she answered, 'It's alright for you – you went to university.' It's not that my auntie had homophobic beliefs; she just didn't know anyone who was gay and didn't understand.

Many years on, their mother–daughter relationship is good. But it's not always the same story for many LGBTQ+ people and their families, because often families don't know – or think they don't know – a gay person or a trans person or a non-binary person. They have no connection with the real people behind these labels they read about in newspapers.

When we spoke to Carl, whose story is in this book, I remembered my aunt's reaction to my cousin coming out. When Carl told colleagues in the RAF he had a boyfriend, one of them asked him, 'What do you do when you're together? When I go home for the weekend, my girlfriend and I will cuddle up on a sofa and watch TV. What do you do when you're gay?'

All ignorance isn't built on hatred. I know many generally kind, well-educated people who just don't understand the trans or non-binary experience that so many others go through. They believe 'this sort of thing didn't used to happen'. Of course, it did. Even the most cursory search online reveals a huge archive of historical examples. Remember, it wasn't too long ago that highly intelligent people truly believed that women didn't possess the intellectual capacity to vote! Widely accepted public beliefs do change with knowledge and education.

I felt really passionately about starting our podcast *Coming Out Stories*. Emma and I really wanted parents, colleagues and friends to understand the very real journey so many people go on in their lives, just to love and be loved. There is no 'choice' involved. Anyone who really thinks about it knows how ridiculous the idea of 'having a choice' is. Yet for so many, who learn about LGBTQ+ culture through the lens of the tabloid media, that belief is still real. The only real choice here is for people outside the LGBTQ+ community to listen and to understand the truth of people who are part of this community. Believe me, your life will be so much richer!

Of course, there's no definitive guide on what to say when someone comes out to you, but remember that if they do, it's probably because they love you and they care about what you think. They want you to be part of their lives and share their happiness and might also need your support. Sometimes they might be really scared. Can you imagine being afraid to tell someone you're in love? Or what gender you identify as?

If they're afraid, it's because the thought of you not being in their life is unbearable. If you're close enough to someone for them to feel that way, then you no doubt love them too. Remember that. They are still the same person you love.

I'm always a bit discombobulated when people say to me, 'I can't bear to think about what they do in the bedroom.' I don't know about you, but I don't spend a lot of time thinking about the sex lives of *any* of my friends and family!

So, if that thought pops into your head (!) why not think about all the things we share, whatever our sexuality? We all feel heart-thumping joy when *that* person walks into a room; we've all felt the desperation of unrequited love, or the loss of heartbreak.

If your child or your sibling or friend is heartbroken, does the gender of the person who has broken their heart really matter? Of course not. Our human instinct towards people we love is to keep them safe and make them feel supported. Trust those instincts. The rest is just a process of learning and understanding.

I'm sure the majority of you reading this have a very definite belief that you're male or female. Imagine having that clarity of belief, but living in a body that told the world something else? Imagine being told to dress and act in a way that felt completely unnatural to you and being too afraid to tell anyone. Non-binary and genderqueer people often accept that it can be hard for cis-gendered people to grasp how they feel. But why dismiss their experience because it's not one you have personally had?

If someone does choose to come out to you as LGBTQ+, do remember that they may not be out to everyone else in the wider world. It may be abundantly clear, of course, but if you're not sure, it's really worth asking. Just a simple 'Have you spoken to your dad/sister/other friends about this?' can ensure you don't inadvertently out someone when they're not ready.

I'm very proud to be an LGBTQ+ ally. But to be honest, I've been the real winner in this relationship – my life has been enriched in ways too numerous to count. If you think about it, the ignorance and hatred of a few could easily have given all straight people a really bad name, and yet still the LGBTQ+ community welcomes us with open arms. We should all feel proud to stand beside them.

Thank you so much to every single brilliant person who has taken time to sit down to talk to us and share some of the most important moments in their lives. We sincerely hope that if you're thinking of coming out, at least some of the stories here will resonate with you. If you feel unsure or afraid, we hope you find some comfort or inspiration. If you're out and proud, we hope you enjoy the love and joy within these pages. And if someone you know or love has come out to you and you don't know how to get your relationship back on track, we hope these stories will help you understand that we all feel the same desire as humans: to love and be loved. That's what binds us. Nothing else matters.

# Asad

'I was told I had to marry a woman.
I lost all hope for my future.'

*Asad grew up in a British Pakistani Muslim household and feared the worst when coming out to his parents. So much so, he packed a bag and had a friend wait outside in his car, ready to escape.*

I think I was about six or seven when I realized. I didn't really know what it was but I definitely knew I was different because I wasn't interested in the girls like my other male friends were. It wasn't until I was just going into secondary school that I found the language, found the word 'gay' and started to really understand sexuality a little bit more. It wasn't until I was 11 or 12 that I thought, 'Yeah, I really am gay!'

The troubling thing for me is that I never really talked about it to anybody. It was only when I got into secondary school that the internet started becoming the thing that it is, so there were no real resources, or people I could talk to, to try and even work through it or understand it. I just knew I was different and I knew it wasn't something I could speak about, because I started to hear words like 'gay' and 'fag', with people (including adults) using them in a derogatory sense. You'd hear them on the street and you'd hear them at football matches. You'd hear those slurs used quite commonly. So, from the signals that I was getting, I just knew I couldn't talk about it or explore it publicly at all.

I can admit that I was homophobic. I hated myself when I was younger. I didn't really understand why this was happening to me. I had no role-models to look up to. I didn't have access to older LGBTQ+ people. So, for me, it was just really lonely. Being religious, I struggled. I genuinely did hate myself. I was homophobic for a very long time.

I tried to not actively be homophobic, but when people at school would say things like 'Oh, that's so gay', I'd join in because I didn't want to be the only person in the group to not say it and therefore be outed. I never joined in with the more aggressive slurs but I also never called it out. I never really intervened or stopped it. I look back now and I'm horrified at that. But for me that was survival. When I was 12 or 13 I couldn't be outed. That would have been the worst thing for me.

I did struggle with who I was. I became very devout at one point. I used to 'pray the gay away' – that saying was literally true for me. I could never really reconcile being gay with my deeply held religious beliefs, even though the teachings of the Quran don't really reference homosexuality. I think the struggle in a lot of Muslim discussions around homosexuality is that the Quran is often brought in or misinterpreted, and then you have the cultural layer on top of that. People outside my community don't realize just how important that cultural layer is. India was one of the most sex-positive societies in the world, you know. But then colonialism imposed Western ideals of sexuality and body image and colourism, and attitudes changed.

I always felt welcome at the mosque. It's always been a welcoming space. But I was hiding a secret and it was always at the back of my mind. I thought, 'Well, if they actually knew what I really was or who I really am, they wouldn't accept me.'

I found it difficult to reconcile my faith and my sexuality. So, for many years I hid it. Back then there weren't the organizations that exist now. There weren't things like Imaan,[1] a great group which helps queer and gay Muslims in the UK. It's a great support and resource, but I never had access to that.

When you're the child of immigrants, particularly Pakistani immigrants with a Muslim background, homosexuality is never brought up. You just do not discuss sex with your parents, whether it's heterosexual sex or homosexual sex – that's just a no-no.

So, I was quite late coming out. I was 22. I'd left the nest at 18 and moved to London for university and to explore my sexuality. I was now a bit more comfortable with it and was trying to understand myself a little bit more – because you've got to admit it to yourself first, right?

I was kind of non-committal in my first years of coming out. I wanted to enjoy it. I also thought that when I finished university I would likely move back home, possibly join the family business and probably have an arranged marriage to a woman. That's what was expected. My sister had that, my brother had that, my parents met through an arranged marriage. That's just part of the culture, so I was convinced that I was going to do it too. I'd readied myself for a life of being married to a woman. It was a struggle. You give up a little bit of hope. You give up a part of yourself, you truly do. You realize how much of a sacrifice, how much of a burden, you're going to have to carry for the rest of your life.

I'm a very outgoing person, very outspoken, but then to hide

---

1   Find them on Twitter @ImaanLGBTQ, Instagram @imaanlgbtqi or at imaan.org.uk

a huge part of yourself really takes a toll on your confidence, on the way you present yourself outwardly to society and to your family. If I'd ever got married, it would have been terribly unfair to my wife. It would have been so, so dishonest to my family, to friends, to my wife and to myself. It would have been terrible, but it's a thing that many people do. Many Muslims still do that.

In the end I made sure I got a job in London, because I thought the more distance I can put between myself and my family, the better. I was trying to find some way to avoid getting married.

But then I met somebody. I fell madly in love with them and they gave me an ultimatum. They told me to come out to my family and tell them about us or leave. Wow! And I thought that was really horrible. To have trust in someone that much and then have them say, 'You need to make this choice or I'm going!' I decided to leave that relationship because I felt the trust was broken, but in the process I had hit rock bottom.

I'd been diagnosed with depression earlier that year and I was struggling to find a way out. So, I decided to come out to my brother first and I did that via text message. That's not the best idea at all, because you don't get to read facial expressions or understand the other person's point of view. With hindsight, I wish I hadn't done it. I wish I'd been able to see their reaction.

In terms of what a gay man is supposed to look like, I was very much the opposite of society's stereotype at that time – I was fat. I love sports. I'm totally into football. I loved R&B and hip-hop music. I was pretty much exactly like my brother; just gay. So, for him it was really hard to reconcile.

His immediate response was bad. He said he felt 'sick'. That was really hard to take. I just remember being in tears on the edge of the bed with a phone in my hand, waiting for a response. I said, 'Why? I'm not a different person. I'm exactly the same person I was yesterday and two years ago. I'm still your younger brother. I've always been there for you. Why can't you be there for me?' We eventually got to a place where he was supportive but we never really talked about it. His big piece of advice was that we couldn't tell Mum and Dad, because it would break them. For the next four or five years we just said that we'd find the right time.

I waited until I was about 24 or 25 and I'd come back to my parents' home from London for the weekend. I'd had it in my mind for a while to tell my dad, because the arranged marriage talk was really ramping up. Twenty-five is considered a really good age to get married and I was getting a few offers coming in. I just felt this was the right time. I wasn't dating but I'd been in two or three relationships and I realized that's what I wanted. I want to be with somebody and I want my family to be a part of that. Family in Pakistani culture is essential. It's so ingrained into the fabric of who you are.

So, it came to Saturday night on this one weekend. It was quite late and I had a bag packed ready to go. I texted my friend and said, 'Hey, can you come round to my house and just park outside, because I might need you.' He didn't even know I was gay. I wanted to come out to my family first.

So, he drove round and was there waiting in the car on the corner. I had my bag packed, because I was expecting the worst. That's the horrible thing about coming out for many of us. Before you come out you assume the worst in the people that you love. That's really hard. The people whom you grew up with, who love you, who are supposed to love you unconditionally – you think that they're going to turn their back on you. The second thing is that you then feel bad for thinking this of them. Thinking so badly of your parents, of your friends – that they would just reject you.

So, I text my dad. It's late and everyone else has gone to bed.

I know that my Mum and Dad stay up late to watch *Zee TV*. They love catching up on their serial Pakistani drama shows in the evenings. It's about half-eleven, and I send him a message. I can hear a 'ping' from downstairs, so he's got the message. I say, 'Can you come upstairs to have a chat?' I'm assuming he'll be really annoyed because he's probably halfway through his romantic drama on *Zee TV*. I get a message that yes, he is coming up. Then I hear the stairs, that slow walk creaking up the stairs. It's probably about 20 seconds, to be honest, but it feels like 20 minutes just waiting for him to come into the room. I'm sitting on the edge of the bed and my dad comes in very cheery, as he always does, with a big smile on his face. I say, 'Pop, can you sit down?' He is like, 'What's wrong?' As I try to say, 'I'm gay', I can't get the word out. So, I then stumble into the arranged marriage thing. I say, 'Well, I can't get married. I can't have this arranged marriage. You know, I'm focusing on my career. I'm trying to get this house.' And bless him – he has an answer for everything. So, he's like, 'We don't have to. You know it doesn't matter about the house. Don't worry about that. You know, there's no pressure to do it. You know, you will find the right person for you.' I just kind of kept making excuses over and over, trying to find a way out – but he's so lovely that he just kept flowing love back at me and saying it's fine. Then I eventually went to the sexual side and I said, 'I can't have children.' He was very concerned. He said, 'Well, what's happened?' He asked me a whole series of questions about that: 'Are you okay?', 'Has there been an issue or accident or something?', 'Do you like boys?', 'Do you like girls?', and so on. I couldn't believe he asked that in the middle of these questions. So, I said, 'Dad, that question you just asked about three questions ago. The answer is yes!'

He looked at me really confused about which question – because he'd asked about ten. I said, 'The one about boys. Yeah, I do.'

I still couldn't say the word gay. There were about five seconds of silence, which felt like five minutes to me at the time, and he just said, 'That's okay. I love you. You're my son. How could I think any different of you?' He gave me the biggest hug. It was actually so beautiful and so not what I was expecting. He said that immediately and then got very introspective and said, 'Oh, I used to make fun of one my friends because his son was gay. Now I realize that *my* son is gay!' So, he immediately felt guilty, which is a good thing because he realized he had done something wrong in making fun of another gay child. He's an amazing man.

My mum just couldn't understand it though. You've got to realize that my parents were born in Pakistan in a very small, poverty-stricken village. They managed to get some money together and move to England, but the society for them growing up was very different to what it is now. They have a totally different set of cultural references. My mother doesn't really understand homosexuality. She still even now thinks it's a choice. And that's not born of hatred. It's born of genuine ignorance. In the environment that she grew up in it's something that's never talked about or referenced. She has very little education. So, how would she have the tools and the language to be able to navigate those conversations with her son?

It's hard not to empathize with people you love, so I don't hold any hatred for my parents. I understand where they're coming from. I just wish there was a little bit more understanding from their side towards me.

There is a happy ending to my story – but with a sad lining. I ended up meeting my now husband about seven-and-a-half years ago.

So, after coming out to my dad and to my mum the relationship was still very good. It actually brought my father and me closer as he got to understand me a little bit more. But the problem is we never talked about it, because it's still taboo to talk about relationships and sexuality.

What sent it over the edge was that I had met this person – this amazing person. And about four or five years in I decided I was going to propose. I told my dad first – that I was thinking about proposing the following week – and that was too much for him, because it was going to become public and it was going to become a thing that now everybody would know. Not just my immediate family, but my extended family, my cousins and the Pakistani Muslim community would know. Previously he hadn't mentioned the fact that his son was gay. It had become our secret between three people – my brother, my mother and my father.

So, in the end my parents didn't come to my wedding. I had a few of my cousins privately say, 'Congratulations, we're really happy for you.' But I didn't have any family there. It's obviously a little bit of a cliché, but I have chosen a family. I have an unbelievable set of friends who were there at my wedding and I've been married to my husband six months now and it's brilliant. Finding somebody like that who understands you, who complements you. We're just really well made for each other! I lived in New York for a while, so my New York family came over, my university people and my London queer people came to my wedding. They all came together and met each other and that was amazing! My chosen family are fantastic and I'm ridiculously lucky to have them. My wedding day was so fantastic. Writing the wedding speech made me realize just how lucky I actually was, and how happy I actually am. And yes, it's not perfect. But as somebody who was born/grew up in the 80s and 90s as a gay British Pakistani Muslim man, I didn't think there was ever going to be a way out. And I mean that quite literally – I never believed I'd even live into my 30s. I have self-harmed in the past. I just never ever thought I'd achieve any sentiment or level of happiness, yet I have done. Despite everything, despite what society has told us or told me, despite the cultural, religious upbringing that I've had, I've still found this wonderful person. I still have an amazing chosen family and I'm happy to have them, I really am. It's taken me years to get there. A lot of introspection, therapy, antidepressants along the way and heartbreak, but I'm here. And that's quite a remarkable, beautiful thing!

'It began to dawn on me that I was probably gay when I was about 12 years old and the thought terrified me. The last thing you want as a kid is to be the odd one out, to be different. I just couldn't imagine how my life was going to pan out. The reality is that I enjoy the most wonderful existence, full of love and laughter, and I'm married to the best wife anyone could dream of.'

**Zoe Lyons**, comedian

# Olivia

'I put my hands over my eyes as I told her, as I couldn't bear to see her reaction.'

*Radio presenter Olivia Jones was an out and proud lesbian at university but struggled with telling her parents, terrified of how they would react.*

I came out quite late to my family.

To my friends I came out at about 15. I think that was really quite a comfortable age where everybody was discovering boys and how exciting they were. I went to an all-girls school, so I felt quite obviously gay. I didn't fit into what everyone else was doing.

At my school I did feel like the only gay one. I was definitely the only one that expressed it at school. To start off with it felt really uncomfortable. I felt like I had to hide it. I developed this overwhelming crush on the girl that I sat next to in biology. Ironically, her name was Hope and there was none. There was just none at all!

It was a real playground crush. I used to take her stuff to make her talk to me. I used to wind her up. I used to do all the things that you do when you have a massive crush on someone and you don't know how to express it. That drew attention to me because people would say, 'You're being quite weird towards her.' That was when I was 15 and, as I said before, that's probably when I came out.

People definitely picked up on it and I felt like the odd one out. But luckily I was part of a group where we were all the odd ones out. In it we had the rocker, the one that was into hardcore metal, and we had the one that was really intelligent and went to Cambridge. You know, we were all misfits that ended up hanging out together. And so being part of that group, I felt like I could hide a little bit more, because it was like 'We're all weird and we own it!'

And they accepted me, 100 per cent. My mate – the really intelligent one that went to Cambridge – her parents had this really big house. They used to go away on holiday and let her do whatever she wanted, which was really bizarre. She used to have three-day house parties and I remember specifically the first day and not everyone was there yet. It was just the three of us: me, her and another girl.

We were drinking whatever we could find in the cupboard and I just burst into tears. I was quite a weepy drunk before I really accepted my sexuality. Now I'm the happiest drunk. I think it's weird. It must have been like a subconscious thing that it just came out. I remember just bawling my eyes out. But my friend said to me, 'It's alright, it's fine. You're all good. We've got your back. It's not going to be a problem. It's going to be fine. It's alright.'

So, it was really cool at school, but I hid it for ages from my parents.

My sister had gone off to university and was about to head out to New Zealand, but before she went we found ourselves at a hen do. We had a few drinks and I think it gave me Dutch courage. I took her to one side and said, 'Look, I'm gay. I'm really struggling with it. I don't know whether to tell Mum and Dad. I know that Mum's going to have a terrible reaction to it. I don't know how Dad will feel about it.'

The reason I knew that my mum would have a bad reaction? She's bit of a *Daily Mail* reader – that stereotype. So, I was really, really scared about it. And my sister said, 'No, 100 per cent, I've got your back. It's all cool.' But she was going to New Zealand in a month, for a year, and so I didn't pluck up the courage before she left.

So, then I went to university and found out that I could be who I wanted to be from day one. I could come out on the first day of university, which I did. However, I was forced out ever so slightly because around about that time 'No homo' was a thing. I don't know whether it was a Kanye thing. I definitely remember Ed Sheeran used to say it. It was when a guy would give another guy a compliment but they didn't want to come across gay. So, they would say 'No homo' afterwards, and the boys started doing it at university. It was maybe a couple of days in and I said, 'Guys, you're going to have to stop doing that, because I'm gay and it's quite offensive', and they all said, 'I'm so sorry, I'm so embarrassed!' You know, they were just doing it because it was a popular thing at the time, but the apology totally made up for it. These guys didn't think about what they were doing.

If they had reacted badly, it would have made me go, 'Okay, we can't be friends', but they had a great reaction and I had an amazing time at university. I think the first year was really coming to terms with what it meant to be gay. I enjoyed the dating scene and our university had a monthly gay night called 'Tease', which was such a celebration of LGBTQ+ life.

But still I hid it at home. I remember I was back from

university in the summer of my third year and I was seeing a girl that I'd met online. We'd been out for a date and had a lovely time and she'd parked her car near where I live. So, she was just getting into her car and we had a kiss goodbye. But it was outside my house and my mum was stood at the window. I looked at the girl and I said, 'I think my mum just saw me kiss you!', and she said, 'She could have arrived just afterwards, you don't know.' I went inside and my mum just avoided me. She didn't talk to me for a couple of hours. So, I think she knew but she didn't bring it up and still I didn't come out.

A couple of weeks after that we were talking about a friend of mine from school that I'd seen on a dating website. I don't know whether I was trying to provoke the conversation but I brought it up and I said to Mum, 'Do you know that "so and so" is gay?' And she said, 'Oh, right.' And I said, 'Yeah, it must be really hard to be gay.' And then she said, 'Do her parents know?' And I said, 'No, I don't think so, but it's quite difficult to come out to your parents.' And she said, 'Right.' Then there was a big silence where we stared each other from opposite ends of the sofa.

My mum and I have a very similar personality in that when we are awkward we make a joke that bursts the bubble. She said, 'Are you pregnant?' And I said, 'No.' And she said, 'Are you gay?' And I said, 'Yeah.' And I remember being so terrified about how she was going to react that I put my hands over my face because I didn't want to see. I didn't want to see what her instant reaction was. Regardless of where she was going to be in six months' time, accepting me and loving me or whatever. That instant reaction you have; that face can't lie – if they're disappointed, if they're hurt, if they're upset – and I just knew I didn't want to see it. So, I just covered my face and burst into tears. I remember I had my knees up on the sofa as well. I kind of went into the foetal position. I guess that body language says everything. You know,

I was just so defensive, like a hedgehog. I wasn't ready to face the consequences.

But Mum ran towards me and she put her arms around me, and she said, 'Don't cry. It's okay. It's okay. How long have you known? Does anyone else know?' Obviously at that point you have to admit, 'Yeah, my sister knows. She's known for ages. My friends know. And because my friends know, their parents know.'

The hardest thing for me has been my mum not knowing something so personal about me, when everyone else knew. She had a right to know. I could see that she was hurt, but she put me first. She put how I felt first, and she could understand why I had hidden it.

Now, she doesn't remember saying this and she has since apologized, and she feels so bad about it. I think it hurts every time I repeat it, but it's good for people that are considering coming out to know that sometimes parents make statements that they do not end up standing by. My mum said to me once that she would be disappointed if I was gay. That sounds like she was disappointed in me, but she actually meant she would be disappointed that I wouldn't have an easier life. It's because she only wants the best for me and she only wants me to have the most successful life. Actually, her frustration is not with the LGBTQ+ community; it's with the society that surrounds it and the way that we are treated. So, that's something that I held onto and that's one of the reasons I didn't come out sooner.

I said to Mum, 'Can you tell Dad? I just don't think I can go through the emotional stress of doing it again?' And she did. I remember I was upstairs in my room and she went, 'Liv?' And she properly whispered it to me, 'I've told Dad your news!' And then we had dinner together and nothing was said about it! And then I was doing the washing-up and my dad came over to me and said, 'Mum's told me your news and it's not a problem.'

Then he kissed me on the head and walked away and that was that! How phenomenal is that? For a parent to just acknowledge it and move on, and that was it.

I got married recently. My dad walked me down the aisle, which is very patriarchal. I mean, as feminists we are very disappointed in ourselves! My wife said to me recently, 'I think your mum likes me more now that we're married!' And I think that's funny in a way, because when my mum first found out about me dating her, she said, 'Is she a special friend?' She couldn't say 'girlfriend'! But she's since been really, really supportive and I remember that she said my grandparents always made her feel like part of the family straightaway. My wife was the first person I brought home, by the way, and I ended up marrying her, so that's quite a good record! But my mum said whenever we brought someone home, she wanted to embrace them into the family straightaway and make them feel like they were equal. And she did that with my wife absolutely.

For anyone who hasn't yet come out, I think it's normal for humans to think the worst – you always go to worst-case scenario. Let's face it, despite the fact that we live in the 2020s, some people's worst-case scenarios do come true. That is a sad state of affairs. However, time is a great healer and the worst thing that you can imagine usually doesn't end up happening. There will always be people telling you to come out, but that is just not their decision. It's always your decision. It's such a personal thing to do and I think you are the only one that will have to take responsibility for your actions, for the result, and so you do that in your time. I had people saying to me, 'Just do it! Just do it!' and I thought, 'Okay you, sitting up there on your straight throne, telling me what to do! No mate! It's my decision!'

If you get outed, first of all, I'm so sorry that has happened to you. But second of all, it is totally a reflection on the other person, not on you. It is not something that you need to be ashamed of. It is not something that you should feel guilty for or embarrassed by. It is absolutely on the other person.

And you've got to let go of the guilt. I think every single gay person feels guilt at some point for being gay, because no one would choose it. Honestly. No one would choose it. It is a more difficult life. So, why would you choose that? I wish a few more people would understand that. So, if you are gearing up for it, or if you are dreading it, or if you're avoiding it, it's all good. Time... Time will unravel the events.

'I don't think anyone should ever feel pressure to come out! It's a precious and personal choice and everyone should have the opportunity to embark on their own journey, when they are ready! It makes us stronger people in the long run.'

**Michael Gunning**, international competitive swimmer

# Christine

'I told my mum I was a girl when
I was just four.'

Credit: Kieron Chrisham Pholux Foto

*Christine Burns, MBE, author of* Trans
Britain, *has been at the heart of the Trans Rights movement since
the early 90s. She also has one of the earliest coming out stories we
have heard – she was just four when she told her mum she wanted to
grow up to be a woman. But it took another 20 years until she came
out to them again.*

I have come out so many times. Where do you start? I was born
in 1954 and about that time a lot of stories about trans people
started coming into the mainstream. I was about four and a half
and I remember telling my mum that I wanted to grow up to be
a lady. She just brushed it off and made a little bit of fun out of
it. I got quite upset and ran off upstairs.

Both my parents treated it very lightly and I realized that
this wasn't something you said. So, I immediately went back
in, because you get these signals from the grown-ups around
you, and from school as well, that there are certain things you
don't say. And, of course, this was the 1950s. They wouldn't have

had any points of reference really, not like parents might have today.

Fast forward to when I was 12 years old. It was 1966 and my parents had a pub. I used to have a lot of time on my hands, which actually was quite good because it meant that I could dress up if I wanted to without anyone catching me. My elder sister, who's 10 years older than me, had left home many years ago and quite a lot of her clothes were still around. So, I actually had a complete wardrobe to play with and I had hours and hours on my own.

I remember my dad used to send me to get the Sunday papers. And one day, as soon as I got to the newsagents, there was a sign outside that said, 'My life as a woman'. This was the story of April Ashley and it was in the papers. So, I grabbed the papers and ran home. I can picture the exact scene in the kitchen, kneeling on the carpet. My parents are downstairs serving customers and I'm reading all about April Ashley. And in that moment, I discovered that I wasn't the only person like me in the world. I did actually worry that I was uniquely freakish and that there was a name for people like me and (because I was reading it in the *News of the World*) that it was a very bad thing to be. I knew that this was something that would bring the sky down on me if anybody knew.

At school they quite often called me a girl and they had a girl's name for me. I think children – actually before the adults – were reading me because of my mannerisms and because of the way I talk. I was quiet and I was bookish, so I got bullied. I went through a lot of schools. That was the only thing that saved me, to an extent. My parents were moving around a lot because they were buying houses to renovate and so I was constantly experiencing new schools and having to be sussed out by new groups of children. I very quickly became the kid that got bullied.

You realize you've got something that makes you, in the rest of the world's terms, a freak. Therefore, you don't want to be that. The first thing I wanted to do was grow up and be ordinary.

The next step was when I was 18 and left home. We were in the southeast of England and I moved to Manchester to go to university in 1972. I arrived at the time that the Gay Liberation Front in Manchester was beginning to find its feet, but the city was still very straight. I remember my very first night in a hall of residence and the chair of the residents' association stood up at dinner and gave instructions about the places to avoid, which were essentially the precursors of Canal Street. He was telling us to avoid the gays.

I was very covert and very amateur back then. I got a car and that meant I could get away into remote places where I could just be me. I feel ashamed of how ashamed I was, but there were no role-models. In 1974 a group had just been set up in Manchester on Camp Street. I had no difficulty in remembering the address! So, I went there and I sort of staked it out from across the road and saw people coming and going. Back then, people were referred to as transsexuals rather than transgender. My heart was going thump, thump, thump, thump in my chest. Eventually I plucked up the courage and knocked on the door. I went in and there was a back room and I remember it was fairly seedy. There was a settee with springs coming out of it, and cracked mugs for the tea. It was very much about people just being relieved to meet somebody like themselves. I realized I could talk to people and actually find some connection. Being able to go there and see that group periodically was a safety valve. It was an opportunity.

I started to question whether this group was for me though, because it was dominated by people who just cross-dressed once a week. It was their relaxation and they sat around talking about steam engines and computers. But transgender people were such a small community that beggars couldn't be choosers. We didn't have our own groups.

One of the things I thought to myself was that maybe I could just be a cross-dresser and I could contain it to the occasional evening and then put it away in a box. Maybe that would be enough and wouldn't mean the potential of losing my friends, losing my job, losing everything. I was enjoying myself. I was doing my research. I liked the people I worked with, but I didn't think anybody would accept me if I actually said, 'I'm going to transition to be a woman.'

Then in 1976 I came very close to the first attempt to transition permanently. I actually found a doctor, and quite scarily the doctor just said, 'Yeah, we think you're transsexual.' Then he said, 'There's somebody I can refer you to. Come back next week if you want me to do that.'

That was so scary I actually gave up my PhD study and ran away! It meant facing up to everything. I was pretty sure what the prospects would be. I wouldn't be able to continue being a research student or go on to be a lecturer. So, in a way, actually it became a self-fulfilling prophecy, because I ran away from all of my career prospects! Once you've acknowledged to yourself that much, that this is what you are, you can't put it back in the box.

Going away was an act of desperation. I wanted to make another start. So, I got a job with a computer company in Windsor. I didn't actually stay there for very long because it was very lonely. I ended up managing to engineer it within the same company to come back to Manchester, so I could be near the people I'd left.

The next stage was I got so desperate that I actually told my parents again. I was trying to cut off my lines of escape from myself. So, I got very drunk one night and about three o'clock in the morning I rang my parents.

For some reason I always seem to do this stuff kneeling on the carpet with the phone in front of me. My father answered the phone and I said, 'I've got something to tell you. I want to be a girl. I want to be a woman.' I laugh looking back, because he said, 'You'd better speak to your mother!' So, she came on the phone and what she said to me has always stuck with me. She said, 'Darling, we made you and whatever you are, we'll love you!'

I'd actually become quite distanced from my parents. I don't know whether that was because I was angry with them because I perceived that they would put up a barrier. At that moment, on that phone call, I thought that I was about to lose my parents, that I might not ever see them again, because that happens so often to people. That's a mark of my desperation. I felt I'd come to the point where I was actually prepared to lose my parents. I went down to see them in Kent. I remember we spent the evening sitting having drinks and chatting and talking about everything. And my mum just immediately sort of clicked into 'this is my daughter'. They were incredibly good at that and I'd completely misread them.

The chances were that my colleagues wouldn't know what to do with me. So, I changed my work to being self-employed. I set up as an IT consultant, on the basis that I couldn't sack myself! I set about making myself so essential to my clients that they would have to think twice about just letting me go.

When I did finally take the final step of saying, 'Okay, I'm going to be Christine forever', one of my clients had a company meeting and the managing director told the staff. He said, 'Look, this is happening to this person and we are going to accept her. And if anybody has any trouble with that, you come and see me.' So, I have been incredibly fortunate over the years that all the terrible things I knew could happen didn't happen. I've been terribly lucky to have been associated with people who have acted like grown-ups.

The thing about being trans is you cannot avoid coming out – unless you move overnight, people are going to know that something has changed. I think you can succeed in being gay or lesbian for a very long time without telling your colleagues. In the companies that I dealt with, as soon as they knew Christine was trans, I would have the gays and the lesbians in that company coming and buttonholing me and making me their friend, but they weren't out! They were observing me with real interest to see how their colleagues would behave towards me.

I was very fortunate in that very quickly I was able to pass and go invisible and be in a line of work where I was constantly meeting new clients. In a way, it was simpler. And I was living in a very conservative part of Cheshire as well, so I felt it was safest to be in what we call 'stealth'.

And then a number of things started to happen. I realized that if somebody wasn't standing up and doing something, then it was never going to get any better. One of the characteristics of trans history is that from the setting up of the very first support group in 1966, all the way through to the end of the 80s, nothing had progressed (other than people having support groups where you could go and meet people and you could talk).

There didn't seem to be any way to change things. Normally, if there's a social wrong, then you might go to the press and somebody will take up your cause. Well, the press wasn't interested in that. They've got a way of writing about us and it was 'The freaks on Sunday'. You could go to an MP, but this was the time of Section 28 and there were no votes for MPs getting involved with trans people. So, how do you begin when everything is against you?

I got involved in the trans rights movement in 1993. But it

wasn't until 1996 that the European Court of Justice ruled that it was sex discrimination to dismiss somebody because they were undergoing, or had undergone, gender reassignment. That meant that the new Labour government in 1997 had to do something about it. And as a result of that we got the first legislation to protect trans rights.

I was awarded an MBE for my campaigning work because I got involved with civil servants and ministers to help craft the Gender Recognition bill. For a few years at the beginning of the noughties our job really was to make sure that the government could get it through Parliament without getting a scratch on them. And so, I think a grateful government and a grateful Queen decided to give this award to me and my colleague Stephen Whittle (who was awarded an OBE).

When Stephen and I decided to accept our honours, it wasn't really for our egos. It was to say, 'Okay, if we accept these, we are acknowledging the people who devoted their spare time to the rights of this tiny group of people. That was something that was worth doing. It was something worth honouring and we have come a long way.'

What advice would I give to a young person struggling and trying to come to terms with their gender identity? Well, I guess I could say, 'Look at my own life. I didn't have the best of beginnings, but see where I've ended up! You can be the person that you're destined to be. But don't feel that it all has to happen straightaway, take your time.' I know that's a very difficult thing to say to a young person, but actually it's important to spend time, like I did, to actually organize your employment so that you're not going to become destitute. You have to plan. You can say, 'Okay. I'm going to do this, but what are the steps?' Treat it as a project and along the way, of course, learn about your own history.

Trans history is a really inspiring story because it's full of so many really good role-models. If you read about that, then I think you'll know how to manage your own transition. It's a really exciting journey. I think the message of hope would be that you might think of being trans as being a bit of a bummer, that it's a bad hand to be to be dealt, but actually it isn't! That's because we get to do something that the vast majority of human beings never get to do. Most human beings get issued a gender when they're born and they're supposed to stick with that. So, they'll grow up living their entire life experiencing only half of what it is to be a human being.

Although I didn't much enjoy experiencing the other half, I think I understand gender on a level that I guess other people may not do, because of that experience of seeing it from both sides. Because of the person it's made me, because of struggling through hard times and being surprised by what I could do, I would never trade it!

People might say, 'Wouldn't you perhaps wish that you'd just been born a girl and grown up and done the usual stuff?' Well, yeah, that's one way of living a life. I won't decry it because that's what most of the population gets to do. I actually thought I'd been dealt a really bad hand, but actually it's turned out to be such an exciting journey of discovery that I'm a better person than I could ever have been, had I not been challenged in this way.

'I want you to know it will all be okay. Those first steps may seem huge, but you will look back in years to come and think "I did it" – I looked in the mirror today and said the very same to myself, then walked away with the biggest smile.'

**Stephanie Hirst**, broadcaster

# JP

**'At first, I'd just come out to myself, telling my reflection in the mirror "I'm gay!"'**

*Born and raised in a traditional Latino household in Los Angeles, JP felt he wouldn't be accepted in his community or culture for being a gay man.*

I knew very early on that I was not like the other boys at school. There were boys at my apartment building that I was very affectionate with at a very young age. Looking back at it now, I was a lot more effeminate than I let on and so it was a lot more obvious to people. I grew up with my sisters and so I've always been more comfortable around women. I think I've always felt that I was different, that I stood out.

At first, I thought it was because I was Latino and everyone around me was white or Filipino. I was born and raised just north of LA in the San Fernando Valley. My mum is Colombian and my dad is Peruvian. My dad was a construction worker. My mum was a stay-at-home mum. In that respect, it was a very traditional, mainly Spanish-speaking, very religious Latino household.

I was at a Catholic private school from kindergarten to 12th grade. I think I came out to myself eventually in high school, but the Church and organized religion definitely didn't help the situation. I would pray every time I said a bad word. It was tough because I put a big pressure on myself to modify my behaviour, to not be as Queenie as I knew I was, because all the boys made fun of me.

Once you start really thinking about the gravity of what the 'sin' is, you almost feel like you're fucked, like you're going to hell, like there is no recourse for you, because that's basically what the Bible says. The Catholic religion believes that if you are gay and you're not in a heterosexual relationship, then you're going to hell. To think that at a young age is really devaluing.

I was very much on the down-low about it. When I turned 14 or 15, I remember we got our first computer. I had nobody to talk to and so I took to the internet and met strangers online. In retrospect, I put myself in sketchy situations. But that was the only way that I felt like I could learn. I needed to get to people who were like me.

There was no one at school. The other boys would just copy my mannerisms and call me names. I lost count of the number of times I heard the word 'faggot'. It would make me hate them and then hate myself for giving them ammunition to do that to me. There wasn't any physical abuse but there was a lot of emotional abuse. It was a lot of shit to take. I remember not being able to do anything but cry, and that reinforces the sissy image. I couldn't go home and tell my mum that they were making fun of me for being gay because then that's me admitting that I'm gay. So, yeah, it was kind of tough at school.

I got my driver's licence when I was 16, and I think that changed a lot because it gave me a lot of freedom. That's when I started meeting guys. That's when I started thinking, 'I need to come out to myself.' So, I said it out loud to myself in the mirror. I had to, in order for me to be able to practise and say it out loud and really own it. There were times I screamed it out loud! That's because you just need that release, you need it to be okay and for the world to know. I had to reclaim myself and this was a way of not letting any of the bad names or rejections or anything else affect how I would move forward as my true self.

The first person I told was my best friend Zara. We were talking about what careers we wanted to have and I said something like, 'What would you say if I wanted to become an astronaut?' Then I said, 'What would you say if I was gay?' And she said, 'I wouldn't say anything.' So, I didn't confess right then and there.

The first few times it was really emotional. In my family I came out to my sisters first. In a way, they always knew, because I would tell them how to dress up their Barbie dolls and I would organize their closets!

I was the first boy, and in the Latino family there were a lot of expectations placed on me. My parents were immigrants. So, education was really massive and there was a lot of pressure on me. For instance, pressure on me to set an example for my sisters, to be the strong man, to lead the family, to carry the name. And I always thought, 'Fuck, I'm gonna fail at that because I'm gay. My parents will never accept me, my sisters will never accept me.'

Just thinking about that was quite scary because these are your people, your blood, who could easily say no and reject you.

But I came out to my sisters and it was amazing. Thankfully, they were really, really great and we're the best of friends now. Next was my mum. Then I went to visit my grandma, because I was actually going to go on a date and see a guy at a cinema, but he lived close to where my grandma was living. So, I went and stopped by and said hi. I think I had waxed my eyebrows and I remember a family member just straight up asking me if I was gay and I panicked. I ran away and went on my date and then I thought, 'Shit, if they know, they're going to tell my mum!' I thought I'd rather be the one to do it. I sat her down and I told her that I wanted her to be in my life and I wanted us to have a good relationship. I said that I wanted to be honest with her but I hadn't been honest with her. Then I told her I was gay. She started crying and cried hysterically for 45 minutes. I almost thought I was going to give her a heart attack.

Then she stopped and asked, 'So, what are you like?' and I thought, 'Okay, interesting question.' And I told her, 'Mum, I'm no different than what you see now. It's not like I take your heels out on Tuesday nights and go gallivanting about the town!' I had to normalize things for her, I think. You know, 15 or 20 years ago, there weren't that many LGBT references in mainstream media. There was *Will & Grace*! In Latin America, gays were really effeminate. There was this guy on TV who was like a fortune teller and everybody knew he was the gayest thing since Christmas. So, I think her idea was that I would be a drag queen or a 'transsexual' because she didn't understand. So, it was about educating her. Really quickly though, she saw that nothing was different and I introduced her to gay friends as well. Seeing how my best friends that I grew up with interacted with my gay friends on a normal level helped her get it in the end.

I also came out to my dad, but with my dad I had an even tougher relationship than with my mum when I was growing up. I came out to him in a fight. I was about to graduate college and he had come over to my flat for something. I was so angry at him and I just said, 'You know, I want to talk to you about my life. I want to have a relationship with you but I can't talk to you about things. I want to talk to you about who I'm dating and I can't!' I'm looking at him and he looks at me and he says, 'So, talk. Who are you dating?' And I said, 'His name's Ron.' And he didn't even bat an eyelid. I threw it out at him, thinking that he would react and he didn't react!

We actually had a conversation about the guy that I was dating but since then, it's not something we've actively discussed. But it's also something I have zero fears about discussing with him.

So, I think I'm very fortunate in that both my parents are quite supportive. They've come to gay bars for my birthdays. I'm now trying to get my mum to come out for Pride to walk with PFLAG.[1] This was a situation where I was really scared that it would go badly, but actually it's been really great.

I still think that in the minority Black communities, Latino communities and Middle Eastern communities, it's harder to come out. I think religion plays a big factor in this. I think there's a macho element that needs to be upheld – it's what we're raised with.

I think as much as you can, follow your heart and trust your gut instinct because that's going to help you gauge how you approach your family and your friends. Be realistic. Hope for the best, but at the same time understand that not everyone might be okay with you in the beginning or further along. But trust your gut and be true to yourself because that is what is going to get you through the good times and the bad.

And talk to the man in the mirror, or the woman in the mirror, or the whoever the fuck you want to be and are in the mirror!

---

1    PFLAG is the first and largest organization for lesbian, gay, bisexual, transgender and queer (LGBTQ+) people, their parents and families, and allies in the USA. For details, please visit https://pflag.org

# Sarah

**'For years, I desperately wanted to be a straight girl.'**

*Sarah was always worried about judgement and persecution, and it took a girlfriend who was happy holding her hand in public to help her get rid of her shame.*

It took me really quite a long time. I really struggled with the word 'lesbian'. I was more comfortable with 'bisexual'. I have been with men. It's not even that I don't find men physically attractive, because I do, I just don't fall in love with them. All my love relationships have been with women. It just got to the point where I thought, 'I've got to stop calling myself bisexual because I really never plan on having a relationship with a man.' I suppose technically I could fall into that category, but it felt more empowering actually to go, 'No, hold on. I need to own this!'

I always knew...I think from the age of six. I remember back then having these feelings for a friend's older sister and it seemed completely normal to me. I had a massive crush and I remember really wanting to impress her.

I felt like I needed to talk to other people I'm close to about this. You know, even at five, six years old, I felt like I had to confess. I remember knowing back then that it was a big deal, despite the fact that we had a lot of gay friends.

When I was really little I went through a phase where I wanted to be a boy and asked everyone to call me Christopher and cut my hair. I didn't speak about this for years and then one day I was talking and the story just came out and I thought, 'Oh my god!' I'd never talked about this publicly and suddenly I was like, 'Well, actually maybe I should because there's no shame in it.'

And actually, a lot of kids have since told me, 'Oh, yeah, I really wanted to be a boy when I was little', or, 'I really wanted to be a girl.' You know, it didn't manifest into anything, but I often wonder whether maybe it might have done had I not been shamed for it (I got really badly shamed).

I'm happy being a woman. I feel like a woman but I can honestly say that had I not had those quite shaming episodes in that very pivotal point in my life around the age of four or five, maybe I would want to identify as a man now? I don't know.

Through the years, I desperately wanted to be a straight girl. I really did. I really wanted an easy life. I thought, 'If I'm straight and I have a boyfriend and he looks good and we look good together, then everything's alright and I'll fit in. I just wanted to fit in.

I didn't ever sit my folks down and 'come out', because I didn't actually want to put a name on it for years. Not really until two years ago. My close friends knew. I mean, I lived with a woman for three years and had a great relationship. I was dating women all through my 20s, but also trying to date men at the same time, hoping that if I just dated the right one or if I just did this or that, you know, somehow I could just… Yeah, I really wanted to be straight.

I was talking to my ex-girlfriend the other day as I realized that she contributed a lot to that shame falling away. I was the first woman she had been with, and I remember saying to her, 'I hope this isn't weird for you, I know it's a big deal when it first happens.' And she said, 'No, on the contrary. I think it's really beautiful and natural.' And I thought, 'Oh! Maybe it is!' She instilled that in me. She would take my hand in public, which is something I could never do, even in my long-term relationships. I was terrified of judgement. I was terrified of abuse and persecution. She would just take my hand, and suddenly I looked around me and thought, 'Actually, maybe this is really cool. This is alright. I think I can let this shame go.' It just slowly started to slip away. The more I behaved in a way that was suggesting I don't have any shame, the less shame I felt.

I never used the 'G' word and then never used the 'L' word. I absolutely hated the word 'lesbian'.

So, coming out to mum, I remember just telling her as a teenager that I thought I had feelings for another girl, and that was it really. It was the same with my dad and my step-mum. I've been really, really lucky with my family – they've always been wonderful about it.

When I was 18, I had been dating this South African girl. It was a crazy fling and I mentioned it to my step-mum. I was visiting and was like, 'Maybe you could drop it into conversation with Dad.' She did, and then when we were all sat down one day, Dad said, 'Listen, Sarah, I literally I don't care who you date. As long as they treat you well and you're happy, I really don't care. I want to make that really, really clear.'

As a child, those are the exact words that you want to hear.

If anyone else still feels shame, I would say that it is an inside job. Once you've faced it with yourself, then it's much easier with everybody else because you don't care what people think. But if you haven't dealt with your own feelings, if you are carrying any shame, then you're always going to care what people think. Shame is a big one. It's not something you can just shake off. So, if you are unfortunate enough to have been shamed and to be carrying these sorts of deep, heavy weights, go and talk to someone to help you process it, I'm always an advocate of that. Maybe even talk to a professional who can help you just unpick it in your mind and in your heart, so you can release it, because it's completely unwarranted shame. You've got nothing to feel ashamed of. Who you are is beautiful, and love is beautiful.

'My advice is for family and friends! I was so lucky with mine, because all we have is love and support for each other. They just want me to be happy above anything else, and if you love someone, that's all you should want for them! It's really quite simple! Leave judgement behind. And let your LGBTQ+ loved one be authentically themselves. Just like you get to be without fear of hate/rejection.'

**Stephen Bailey**, comedian

# Oskar

**'I take the view with my trans identity, that unless you are going to get into my pants, I'm not really interested in coming out to you.'**

*Oskar grew up in Trinidad and identifies as trans-masculine but non-binary. In terms of his sexuality, he identifies as pansexual. He struggled with drug addiction, homelessness and mental health problems after suppressing the urge to transition for 20 years.*

How I identify is constantly evolving. At the moment I identify as trans-masculine non-binary. Sexuality wise, I pretty much identify as pansexual. But I do tend to say I'm bisexual, just for the ease of not having to have a long conversation about it!

I think it's important for people to realize that identity is really an internal thing, not necessarily how you look to other people. For me, non-binary is that you see gender on a spectrum, which is basically how I've always thought of gender, and so nobody is absolutely male or absolutely female. There's always a mix of the two. There's also the complication that gender is also a collection of ideas about how you look or react to other people.

The idea that I'm me in isolation to the world is a bit ridiculous. So, I am 'me' in contact with people and situations at any given moment. So, my identity is as fluid as my gender.

I've had a series of coming out stories! Initially, I came out as a lesbian. As I was growing up in the 70s and 80s, there was very little language or information about identities other than heterosexual, binary gender identities.

I was born in the Midlands in the UK, and then when I was about four we moved to Trinidad in the West Indies, which is where my father's from. It was in many ways idyllic. It's a beautiful island and it's possibly one of the few places in the world that really celebrates a mixed-race identity, which I have.

We left Trinidad when I was 11, but I remember before we left we started to hear the stories coming out about the AIDS crisis. That was probably the first time I'd ever really come into contact with the idea that a man could love a man, and a woman could love a woman. It was confusing and also exciting because I was starting to recognize something of myself in the stories of the people that I was hearing about. But also, there was this terrible thing happening, and essentially there was lots of rhetoric about whether or not this was something that was supposed to happen. People would say things like 'It's god punishing gays' and that kind of stuff.

School in Trinidad was intense. I was bullied a lot in school for being different. I was a very masculine girl who hung around with boys and didn't really do lots of 'girls' stuff'. I knew I was different; I knew I wasn't the same but also at that point I hadn't really got the language for a lot of how I was identifying.

I was questioning my gender from the time I was a child. I basically thought I was a boy up until primary school, but then I had to wear a dress because I was a girl (up until that point I didn't have to). I hated it. I wore shorts underneath my dress as a way of protecting myself. But yeah, I hated it. When I was teased for being in a dress, that was even more upsetting because I was already vulnerable in a dress!

I had to wear a dress for my First Holy Communion. That was horrific. I mean, I only wore it because my mum had made it, but it was a terrible, terrible time! And then I had one dress that I had to wear on my sixth birthday. It was horrible! And I think that was probably the last time my mum made me wear a dress outside of required parameters.

In terms of sexuality, I came out quite early. It was just after I moved back to the UK, when I was about 12, and my mum was okay with that. She said, 'You're part of the family and that's not going to change.' My dad was okay about it too. Basically, my mum told him, and I think it's quite amusing because she went with 'hard news then soft news'. She said, 'Your daughter's addicted to drugs and she's a lesbian.' And my dad was like, 'I don't care who she sleeps with as long as she gets off the drugs.'

I got into substance abuse at a very young age. I was just about 11, 12 years old when I came back to the UK. So, I came back from what was a very strict, conservative school environment where you stood up if teachers entered a classroom. I then found myself in a high school in one of the more challenging parts of London, where kids would throw things at the teacher and tell them to piss off and that sort of stuff. So, it was a huge culture shock for me. Also, just arriving back in the UK, with the levels of segregation and racism that existed compared with the country that I had just come from, was a huge shock.

I made some friends and within the first year we started experimenting with drugs. It was anything I could get my hands on, but mainly pot. Looking back on it now, I see that it was a way of me coping with what was going on, but it wasn't in any way helpful to me.

I was involved with drugs all the way up to the age of about 30, when I decided I just couldn't do this anymore. I was just using stuff to numb and cope with what was going on. I'd been homeless a couple of times and I was staying at my ex's flat. I had just spent a year with an extreme kind of agoraphobia. I'd been really depressed and I spent about a year on a sofa, refusing to leave the flat. I was basically waiting to die at that point. Eventually, I just had this moment where I asked myself, really honestly, you know, 'If you were going to die right now, would you just let yourself go?'

And the answer was no, I would try and stay alive, and so I thought, 'Well, if that's true, if I really want to live, then I should try and do that!' And that was the start of a very long journey out of mental health and drug abuse issues.

My sexuality was never really an issue for me. My gender identity I struggled with a lot more. The first time I tried to broach the subject with my mum, I was 15. I had just seen a documentary about a trans guy who was going to Amsterdam for the first sort of surgeries that they were offering female-to-male people and I was just like, 'Wow! That's me!' I tried to tell my mum and she was a bit freaked out by it; a bit scared by it. I remember her saying, 'What kind of life are you going to have?' I read her reaction as not being disapproving but just afraid. When you see your parents afraid, that's quite an affecting thing. In fact, I was so affected by her reaction that I just backtracked and kept it secret, which I'd been doing anyway for pretty much my whole life. And so, I just went back to being a lesbian for about 20 years.

This was 1988, so the idea that female-to-male trans people existed was a completely new thing. The only role-model I had at that point was someone called Buck Angel, who was a porn star at the time.

You know, what I needed at that point as a child was just for my parents to go, 'Okay, that's fine. Let's get on with it.' But you know, considering the time it was and what was available to my mother as a single parent, she had a lot to deal with.

Our relationship has just become really amazing in the last couple of years. I've had this conversation with my mum about when I first came out. I basically said, 'I thought you were ashamed of me.' And she just said, 'No, I'm really proud of you. I'm just amazed at what you've done with your life and that you've managed to overcome all of these things!' I think that she was scared. She just didn't know what to do.

I think if I'd come out today as a young person, I'd have much more available to me in terms of role-models. I'd see myself out there and know that what I was experiencing wasn't me going insane. A lot of my journey was coming to the realization that I wasn't making this up; it was real and I needed to do something about it, because that was what was affecting me.

Once I started to deal with my substance abuse issues, I started to really pay attention to the things that were causing me pain. One of the things that just kept coming up was this idea, or this feeling, of being male. Being identified as female was deeply painful to me, so I needed to stop telling myself that I was crazy and start doing something about it.

I wouldn't recommend that everyone takes this route, but I basically used Qigong and Tai Chi and meditation practices. They helped me to build a kind of internal stability that allowed me to keep moving forward, and then eventually I came across a charity that did personal development training. It was kind of like therapy, and they helped me to step away from this idea that I was crazy.

The first thing to realize is that everyone's trans experience is different. So, my experience is completely different to that of somebody who might look just like me – and that's a headfuck for everybody who isn't involved in that experience. Even I sometimes make assumptions about other trans people. I talked to a friend of mine and they basically said, 'The problem is not that you are in the wrong body or you have problems with your gender. The problem is that society doesn't have the scope to understand your experience.' My experience of gender as a trans person is incredibly unique, in the sense that I am not attaching my deep identity to that gender. Now, other people who are trans really identify with their gender; they are very binary and they don't want to be reminded of a time when they were traumatized continually by being identified in the wrong way.

I mean, if you go to a toddler, a little toddler girl, and you go, 'Oh, that's a really sweet little boy!', when it's a girl, just watch how they react. That is what's happening inside of a trans person every time you misgender them. They're just trying to keep that contained in order to function in society.

Coming out to my mum again, there was a series of conversations. It's an ongoing conversation actually with my family because we don't live very close to each other as a lot of my family moved back to Trinidad. So, we spent a lot of time with them getting used to the fact that I was not the same person for them. They're like, 'Oh my god! One day you're like you and the next day you're telling me you're someone completely different!'

For me, I'd had a 35-year journey, which I had done in secret. They had no insight into that. They had to deal with pronouns and different names, and I'm still working with them on that. Different members of my family have different ways of processing it. My mum, who I speak to the most and have the closest relationship with, is very much more in touch with what I'm doing or how I'm being than, say, my dad, who I very rarely speak to because he isn't a very verbal person. So, he still calls me by my old name and still uses my female pronoun. In my world, I allow that because they're the people who've spent their lives with me.

I give my family special dispensation and I do that because they have, in the best way that they can, held me as part of their family their whole lives without any kind of exceptions. That's through being gay. That's through being a drug addict. That's through being homeless. That's through generally being a massive fuckup for a really long time. And if I can't afford some patience and compassion to them while they come to terms with my own identity...

The reality is they haven't said, 'Oh, I never want to speak to you again. You're not part of my family.' Every single one of them has said, 'I don't care what you are, you are part of this family.' So, if they misgender me, I'm like, 'Well, you know, this is tough, but ultimately, unconditional love has to go both ways.'

It's not without difficult conversations about misgendering though. The first time I went back to Trinidad in my masculine body I had to say to my mum and my sister, 'Look we can't do misgendering in public. It's going to be a safety issue for me.' And they hadn't really connected with that. So, it was me explaining to them why it's important, not just 'you have to do this'.

As for coming out to other people, I did it a lot more when I was younger. I do it a lot less now I'm older. I kind of take the view that particularly with my trans identity, unless you are going to get into my pants, I'm not really interested in coming out to you. If it is someone like that, well, I'm very upfront about it. It's not that I hide my trans identity. It's difficult as a trans person – you kind of get squashed between having to come out (because if you don't, you're a dishonest and deceitful person who's tricking people), and then not having to come out (because in what other situation are you expected to divulge intimate details of yourself within the first ten minutes of meeting a complete stranger?). At least give me time to work out if this person will respect me before I tell them something that's deeply personal.

If I meet somebody and there's some interest and a connection, then I will very quickly tell that person that I'm trans, because I'm not the kind of person who's interested in being deceitful. Generally, most people don't care, if they're interested in me. That's the continual surprise for me: that most people just don't really care.

My sexuality has been a discovery as much as my gender identity. I really realized that over the last year. I label myself as a pansexual because I really am attracted to people. I do tend to be attracted to people who are on the more masculine side, so that's androgynous masculine women and generally most men. I'm just attracted to whoever's attractive!

I think the really important thing to understand – and sometimes this can take years – is that you're not broken, there's nothing wrong with you. This journey, whether you like it or not, requires patience. As you allow yourself to accept yourself, more is revealed. So, it's not something that happens very quickly. What you need to do more than anything else is to love and accept yourself. When you can do that, then the pain of other people's difficulties is less affecting and you can see what you need to do for yourself. Just loving yourself is not easy to do and it's often thrown away quite flippantly, but it's a rich journey once you start to get into it.

'I've had two coming out stories – one as a lesbian and now as a trans man. If I could offer any advice, it would be to firstly build a chosen family who will support you in your journey. Secondly, to have empathy for those that don't understand. Finally, never feel like you have to adhere to stereotypes – this is your story!'

**Ca**, drummer, ELM

# Lucia

**'We painted "Lesbians are Everywhere!" on the sides of buildings!'**

*After being outed as a lesbian at the age of 14, Lucia ran away from Ireland and ended up living on the streets in Manchester. She was told by a doctor in the 1960s that she needed a lobotomy because she was gay. She went on to be part of a movement that changed the lives of LGBTQ+ people.*

I was born in a Magdalene Home¹ in Ireland. My grandmother came and took me away from there when I was about three or four and I grew up with her until I was about 14.

I didn't intend to come out in Ireland. My brother found a letter from a girl in my school bag and all hell broke loose in the house. They realized that I wasn't 'right in the head'. That's how they put it.

---

1   Magdalene Homes, also known as Magdalene Laundries, were homes where unmarried pregnant women were sent by their unsupportive families to give birth in secret. With nowhere else to go, women often lived and worked there for years, and many of their babies were given up for adoption (sometimes without the women's consent).

After she found out I was gay, my grandmother threatened to put me away somewhere, back in another Home. It was a lunatic asylum in Belfast she was talking to me about. That really upset me a lot and she never stopped going on about it and trying to see if she could cure me.

She kept all this from the rest of the family, but in the end I just thought, 'I've got to get away from all this.' So, I decided to run away, as a lot of children did, and still do today.

That was 1965 and I came to Manchester. I found some family there but I only stayed with those relatives for a couple of months and then I left again. Basically, the same thing kept happening. It came out that I was gay and I was afraid that they'd make me go back to a Magdalene Home in Ireland. I thought the best thing to do was for me to just see if I could live on my own.

I came down to Manchester because I'd heard about the gay clubs and pubs. They weren't called 'gay' at the time, though – they were the 'queer' places. I made some friends, but it was just dreadful because I had nowhere to live. So, I lived for quite a long time on the streets with other young gay people that had run away from home for the same reasons as me. There were a lot of gays and lesbians on the street – both boys and girls. We used to huddle together down near Victoria Station under the arches at night. Or every now and again some other gays would put us up if they could. We did that until eventually we found somewhere to live.

There was no place to turn. There was nothing at all for us then. Everyone was just in survival mode. The main thing was keeping warm and not being too hungry, then finding somewhere to wash yourself so you could be presentable walking into the Union pub at night without looking like a tramp!

Once, while I was living on the streets of Manchester, I stole a bicycle. I needed it to try and get where I was going; and someone caught me. Anyway, to cut a long story short, the police arrested me and I ended up going to court. And when I got up in the court, there were about 148 charges against me. I got two years' probation and the rest of the charges were dropped. The judge realized what was happening and it was recommended that I should go and see a psychiatrist because of the 'gay thing'. They said that they had a cure for it. They thought that I was off-kilter and that I was suffering from depression and it was all due to the fact that I was gay. I mean, I was only a kid at the time. I think I was coming up to maybe 15 or 16.

Anyway, I went to see the psychiatrist and the things he was asking me really shocked me. Coming from a Catholic background, they seemed absolutely awful. They were dirty questions. He then started talking about a lobotomy, but I had never heard of it. I'd never heard of a lobotomy! And he was sitting behind this big mahogany desk and he was talking about all these experiments that he wanted to do and how I needed to prepare for it. When I realized that he was actually going to tamper with my brain, I just ran out of there. A lobotomy is basically where they cut out a part of your brain that they think is the cause of your homosexuality. And it leaves you like a cabbage or numb. You're never the same after that. You become nothing.

I used to spend a lot of time in the Union pub and around Canal Street in Manchester. We had the open mic night, which was brilliant. But there were a lot of unhappy people in there, like me, who had no home and no job. And there were a lot of suicides too. Young people killing themselves. There were also a lot of people that ended up in prison and then came out of prison and had a drug problem. And these were all gay people. So, it became a right dive. But it was our dive and we felt safe in there. But the minute you stepped out of the Union and onto the street, you had to run for your life between pubs and clubs because of all the queer-bashers! That's what they were called. And we also had to run from the police at that particular time too. It started to depress me, and it was a life that I (along with a lot of other young people like myself) didn't think we could put up with any longer.

So, we started talking. But none of us knew what to do or how we could change anything or even change ourselves. We were a mess. I remember thinking all the time that this has to change! It had to change because we were losing too many young people through suicide. And a lot of kids, who we knew were gay, went missing and we never heard what happened to them. It was just starting to really get me down. I was at a really low ebb.

So, when one night I heard a conversation at another table about the Gay Liberation Front, I was interested! I didn't even know what 'Liberation' was! I knew nothing about nothing! But when I heard my friend Angela talking about all this Gay Liberation stuff, I asked her if I could just sit down and have a listen to what they were saying. I thought it was really interesting. The movement was so important to me because it was all about changing things for everybody.

We ended up painting a lot of buildings with 'Lesbians are Everywhere!' because what we wanted to do really was get noticed. This was the first strategy we had. We thought, 'Let's get everybody talking about lesbians', because nobody was taking any notice! So, you know, you light the spark and see what happens.

I didn't want anybody else to go through what I went through. I was very conscious of that.

I think we should all look back at what people had to do to achieve what we have today. It didn't come easy. It had to be fought for on all levels.

It's hard to recognize that Manchester today. I like to go the

Manchester Pride parade every year and just stand outside the Union pub. And I cry. But I cry with happiness. Because I think, 'Look at what has happened since the day we had that meeting in the Union in the late 60s. Look at what's happened since. It's wonderful!' And this is why I would urge all gay people to get out there and enjoy their life and be the best that they can be.

# Jacob

**'Nobody understands what being non-binary means.'**

*Jacob took a long time to come out to themselves, and then meticulously planned coming out to their mum.*

Well, I officially came out in September 2017 – to myself. I came out in my own head and then it took me well over a year to actually come out to my family and most of my friends.

The process was very much discovering what I'd always sort of known but never been able to put a label on. That may be why I'm quite fond of labels now, because before I found the term, I didn't understand any of the things that I was experiencing. Like going to the toilet, for example. I hated going to the toilet in public. Going to the men's was like my worst nightmare. Everyone's told me it was because I was shy, but I never quite felt it was because of that. Now I look back on that and realize why I felt bad: because I don't feel like either male or female.

I define as non-binary. Or genderqueer. Whichever anybody prefers. I prefer non-binary, but I do sometimes use genderqueer if people are a bit like, 'What's non-binary?'

For a lot of people, it's a new term. It's not a new thing, but it is a new term. So, for many people I come across, I'm the first non-binary person they actually know. I always think, 'Really?' I thought there would be more people that come into contact with non-binary people, but apparently not. I'm the first in a lot of cases.

I know some non-binary people who say that some days they do feel quite male and other days they do feel quite female, but to me that is more genderqueer or gender fluid. But I always feel sort of slap-bang in the middle of gender. I never feel male. I never really feel female. I'm just here in the middle.

On my way to figuring this out, it was very confusing because I didn't understand what I was feeling. And when you bring sexuality into that as well, it's a whole other board game, because homosexuals are attracted to people of the same gender. So, how does that work? If you are non-binary, how do you define your sexuality? I'm still discovering things about sexuality and I'm still researching stuff because I'm very much interested in how it all links together. For me personally, I lean towards attraction to men and males but also to male-presenting people. The term for that is 'androsexual', which just means I am attracted to men or male-presenting people. I'm attracted to masculinity over femininity.

As I'm non-binary, I prefer to be called 'they' or 'them' rather than 'he' or 'she', but it's hard for people to understand this. I get misgendered all the time. It happened today, I went to see a counsellor for the first time and I was too scared to actually tell the counsellor. It's just one of those things. I still can't bring it up with my GP because I just don't know if they'll get it, and that's scary. It's a really scary thing to think, 'Should I?' I really want to, but my heart's just like, 'I can't bring myself to explain this again.' So, a lot of the time I end up not doing it because I'm just working one step at a time.

My mum is really trying to understand and we've got to think about telling my grandparents eventually. It does feel at the moment though that it is the younger generation teaching older generations about non-binary and about gender fluidity.

The conversation with my parents was tough. Really tough. Especially after what my mum said about two years before I came out as non-binary to her. I went on a young campaigners' event with Stonewall[1] and I came back and she asked me about how many boys and girls were there and I said, 'Well, there was a mix of people. Some of them were non-binary.' And she said, 'You can't change the world in a day! This is just how it's always been: boys and girls.' I just stayed quiet because I was only about 17 and I was really new to the concept and unsure.

Then two years down the line, here I am, and I've come out to her. I had to plan it. It wasn't just a coming out. It was a proper plan and I had articles ready that I thought she would really understand. So, I sent her an email and I had these articles attached and she responded, saying she was going to read them. So, she did read them and she really, really clicked with the articles. They really worded it better than I ever could have done in person.

So, yes, I emailed my mum. I came out by email. It was a really difficult decision to email because I really wanted to do it in person. But at the same time I didn't feel I could do myself justice by doing it in person. I feel like I could have got too defensive or things could have got confrontational. I was probably blowing it out of proportion in my head but I just needed to know that

---

1   For details of the LGBTQ+ rights group Stonewall, visit www.stonewall.org.uk

she was okay with it. I thought letting her read my email and then read the articles before talking to me was going to be a lot better because of how new the concept is to her and because she's never really come across it before.

Non-binary people have obviously always been around and there's lots of evidence of people being non-binary in certain cultures. But I don't think it's something that people understand, so I feel like I should be that walking bank of knowledge about all non-binary things ever because that's what people expect. They say, 'You identify as it – tell me.' And I'm like, 'It's a very personal thing.' It's such a personal thing. Me being non-binary is going to be different to every other non-binary person because it's not just as simple as not identifying as male or female, although that is the very basis of it.

I've definitely always felt like this. I look back at my childhood and everything about me as a person just points to me being non-binary. Absolutely everything. Like absolutely despising the men's clothing sections whenever I went shopping and stuff like that. I started to wear more female clothes as a way of defying how the world perceived me. Now I don't mind dressing more masculine but I'm definitely androgynous. Now I just choose things that I think look nice, no matter what department they are in.

It's still a headache, but there are lots of different ways that I've learned to cope with public toilets. Sometimes it's a case of thinking to myself, 'How do I pass today?', because some days I might look way more feminine and other days I may be way more masculine. I'm like, 'How am I going to pass? Because I need to go to the toilet.' It really panics me looking at the two options. Some people would say to just use whatever, but it's more than that. I have to think, 'Is there anybody who is in there who could hurt me?' That's scary! I've had a few instances where I've heard people come into toilets and so I've just stayed in a cubicle and waited for them to leave. Just in case. It's difficult.

The best bit of advice I always give to my friends who are non-binary is get a radar key because they give you access to the disabled toilets. That kind of suggests that being non-binary we're disabled, and we're not, but it's a definite way around feeling unsafe, because disabled toilets are gender neutral.

As for my mum, she is definitely getting there. I mean, this is quite a fresh coming out – I only came out about four weeks ago. She's really trying and I've already asked her if I can correct her if she misgenders me and she's fine with that. She's started using my name and my pronouns in texts to other people more. So, generally, it's been a really positive response from her because she's really trying and that means so much to me. I know for a lot of non-binary people just seeing people try means so much.

As for other people in my life, I came to university, planning to be non-binary from day dot, making sure I put it on all my forms and everything.

It's still a real experience, because a lot of people don't understand it and a lot of people don't like it as a concept either. Some people can be really quite mean to me about it, saying things like, 'So, what's between your legs?' That's a common one I get. I just say, 'I am not defined by my genitalia.'

It really makes me anxious to just...exist and that's really tough when you're anxious to exist as yourself. Even brilliant allies often fall into the trap of saying 'men and women', and I think, 'Oh great, I don't exist!'

The advice I would give to anyone else feeling this way is to do what feels right for you at the time and it's okay to feel different later down the line. And don't be scared of all the hate that there is in the world. Because there is a heck of a lot of hate but there are always people around to support you, who are wonderful human beings. There are a lot of us in the same boat and we can all make a massive body of people to just exist happily together. I did find that Mermaids[2] (the trans and non-binary charity in the UK) was helpful.

It's a long process, but I think we're getting there. We're getting there slowly. I mean, the world we live in isn't great at the moment, but I hope we can eventually have some sort of positivity towards us as people. Because, we're just people like everybody else.

---

2    For details, please visit https://mermaidsuk.org.uk

'Queers of the world come out. It is the single most important thing you can do to lift the burden of hiding, live an out proud life, increase LGBT+ visibility and help advance queer acceptance: research shows that straight people who know an LGBT+ person are much more likely to support our human rights.'

**Peter Tatchell**, human rights activist

# Emma

**'Are you on drugs, are you pregnant or are you a lesbian?'**

*Emma's dad gave her the option to come out as part of a multiple-choice question. She came out as a lesbian at the end of the 80s and has recently celebrated her 30th 'Gaynaversary'.*

I've spoken to dozens of lesbian, gay, bisexual, trans and non-binary people from all over the world and asked them to tell me their coming out story, so it's only fair that I should tell my own too.

I came out for the first time in 1989, when the world was a very different place. Gay men were being blamed for the AIDS crisis, and tabloids depicted them as predators from the debauched underclass, taking great delight in outing anyone they thought was 'queer'.

Very few pop stars, sports stars or people in the public eye chose to come out. Coming out seemed like a terrifying thing to do back then.

It was the beginning of 1989. I was busy pretending to care

about my A levels, wearing too much eyeliner, listening to The Cure (a lot), and I still hadn't mastered the Rubik's Cube.

In my head I was a rebel, a goth, a poet – but one thing I definitely wasn't was gay. The thought hadn't crossed my mind.

I'd fancied loads of boys, hadn't I? I'd even dated some of them. It being the 80s they had names like Gavin and Kevin, wore lots of denim and loved Jon Bon Jovi.

I think I nearly had sex with Kevin at a party in Bermondsey in 1988 but even I couldn't drink enough Cinzano to go through with it.

My friends went through more boys than Duran Duran had hit singles *and* they were having sex. Actual sex. By the time we were all 17, they'd been through the *Kama Sutra* several times and I was still a virgin.

A lot of people that I've spoken to knew when they were a very young child. But for me, it was a very specific moment. I can tell you that I first realized I was gay on 26 January, 1989. Very specifically, sometime between 10pm and 11pm that night. I was on a coach coming back from a rare school trip to London. We'd been to see *Les Misérables* in the West End. Sometimes I joke that *Les Misérables* made me gay, but what really happened was that on the coach I met someone who changed my life.

I started talking to a girl who was quite new to our school. She was in the year below me and I'd known of her for about a month or two, but I'd paid her no attention whatsoever. And the more I talked to her, the more I thought, 'Why are you so amazing? God, you're an incredible person. Wow, I want to touch you. Oh my god. What's that about? Why do I want so much of you? What's going on?'

My mind was in turmoil because that was the first time I'd ever questioned my sexuality. Something had seismically shifted.

I'm a slow developer but quite a fast mover. To cut a long

story short, I convinced her to stay the night with me and share my bed. Yes, if nothing else, no one can accuse me of taking things slowly.

Then I woke up the next morning and I thought my life was over rather than my life beginning. I really was unbelievably messed up about it. I just thought this was a secret that I couldn't tell people. I felt elated in one sense because I felt like I was truly in love, but I also felt like it was a dirty secret and I couldn't tell anyone. It was like having the best experience of your life but not being able to tell anyone.

It was the 80s, so I really thought it was wrong. I didn't know any other gay people. The British tabloids were full of stories exposing politicians' or celebrities' homosexuality; like it was a dirty secret that needed to be revealed in the public interest. My only gay role-models were Boy George, Jimmy Somerville and Andy Bell from Erasure, and they were all men. Obviously, there was Martina Navratilova, but that was about it, as far as gay women that I'd heard of. It was all a bit unspoken. And it was a little bit scary. And lesbians were a bit scary, and I didn't want to be a scary lesbian! Looking back now, that seems pretty homophobic (people refer to this as internalized homophobia; see the Glossary for a definition). I didn't know anyone who was gay and out and happy, so why would I tell anyone?

My girlfriend felt the same as I did. Both of us were just terrified of being discovered. We both felt very much that this was something that we were going to keep secret. So we did, and we had a secret affair that was actually very exciting, very illicit and felt very naughty and very wrong. I couldn't eat, I couldn't sleep and I couldn't think of anything else but her. I stayed silent for months. Months of having the most incredible love affair of my life but not feeling able to share it with anyone.

But then unfortunately, about nine mounts after it started,

she ended it. She dumped me while 'Only You' by Yazoo was playing, and that ruined that song for me forever!

After I was dumped I was absolutely traumatized, and that ultimately led to my family going, 'What the hell is wrong with Emma?' Of course, I was going through a trauma. I was gay, nobody knew and I was in love and I'd had my heart broken. And it's horrendous when you have your heart broken for the first time. Not that it gets any easier, but at 18 it hit me really hard. I was totally morose and depressed.

In the end my dad took me to one side. He took me into his bedroom for a talk and said, 'Emma, what is wrong with you?' And then, because I couldn't really speak and just couldn't find the words; he gave me a multiple choice of answers! He did the menu of parental nightmares. So, the exact thing he said to me was actually:

'Emma, what is wrong with you?!'

'Are you on drugs?'

'Are you pregnant?'

'Or are you a lesbian?'

And I was so scared, I just went, 'Yeah...one of them.'

Now to be honest, I'm not a parent, but I think I picked the best one! I wasn't on drugs *nor* was I pregnant as a teenager. He clicked straightaway what I meant and what the actual answer was. And it was fine. Obviously, he didn't understand how the world might progress over the next 20–30 years, so he was more upset that I would never be a parent. He was more concerned about being a grandparent, you see. I remember him saying, 'Well, I hope your sister has some!'

So, basically, we cried and we hugged and then, because we're Goswells, we went to the pub and had some beer!

I think my mother knew anyway. I found out later that she'd been through all my love letters from my first girlfriend! It's hard to have secrets around someone like that. I always said she'd make a great investigative journalist, my mother! So, yes, my parents were accepting.

I couldn't even say 'I'm a lesbian' though. I think whenever we talked about it, I would say I was 'gay'. I just hated the word 'lesbian'. It took me about 30 years to cope with saying that word. I guess there were so many negative connotations around it.

I wouldn't say my parents were over the moon and wanted to throw a party and let everybody know. In my mind they were thinking, 'Okay, that's great. Let's just get on with our lives, but don't tell the neighbours.' I think it took them a little while. My mother was convinced that it was a phase for about the first ten years. Thirty years on, she's probably over the fact that it's not a phase now!

After all that, I went travelling for a year and then I went to university. Weirdly, even though I'd been sort of out and gay for a year, when I went to university in Liverpool in 1990 I decided I was going to be straight. I can't believe I tried that! But I still felt the shame. I still felt it. I mean, it's a joke really, isn't it? You can't decide to be straight, any more than you can decide or choose to be gay! At the time I just thought it was too much like hard work being gay. I thought, 'I just want an easy life. I just want to be like everyone else. It's too difficult to be gay. I can't bear it.' And I did try and date men for a while at uni. But me being me, I lasted a week then drank a bottle of vodka, threw up on my neighbour's garden and told everyone I was a lesbian. After a week!

And you know what? Nobody cared. Nobody cared in early-90s Liverpool. I think it's quite telling the way I came out to my best friend, Maria (who's still my best friend today). I was really worried about coming out to her. Apparently (I found out later), I was the subject of several rumours amongst our friendship group. We'd frequently be down at the Student Union and at some point in the evening I would disappear. The rumour was that I was sloping off to go to gay bars! Someone suggested that was a terrible thing to say about me, but Maria just said, 'So what if she is?' I didn't know all this, of course. I didn't know I was being talked about, because they were right – I was too busy hanging out in gay bars!

Eventually, another night in the Student Union, I decided to properly come out to Maria. I'd really built it up. I was sweating. It seems ridiculous to think about it now, but it is a process that you have to go through. You want that acceptance. You want your friends and your family to love you and accept you for who you are. That's why we do it.

So, I really built it up massively inside my head. It was a big deal. I'd had a few beers to calm my nerves. I turned around to her in the Student Union and said, 'I've got something to tell you.' And she went, 'Yeah, whatever... Go on then.' I said, 'Maria, I'm gay.' And she went, 'Yeah, I know, Emma. Yeah, that's fine. Can you just move to the left a bit? Because I think that guy over there is trying to give me the eye. Do you think he likes me?'

She couldn't have been more disinterested in my coming out if she'd tried. This was my big moment, but she was so much more interested in the fact that some bloke on the other side of the bar was giving her the eye! I was so relieved – it was just brilliant!

We build these things up to be so big, and actually most of the time that is the sort of reaction that you get. If you're lucky, people don't really care. People are more interested in their own life. Most people are way more interested in who they're going to have sex with that night than who you're going to have sex with that night!

The thing about coming out though is that it's not just a

one-off experience. Nope, it's something you have to do repeatedly. I guess Elton John or Tom Daley don't get asked about their 'wives' very often; but for the rest of us unknown mortals, people generally assume we're straight. An innocent question from your hairdresser, taxi driver or supermarket checkout assistant about where you're going or who you're going with can lead to a coming out. It's up to you whether you use pronouns when referring to your partner or whether you mention that you're off to a well-known gay club that evening. It's something you'll find yourself doing on a regular basis for the rest of your life; and the more you do it, the easier it gets. The more we all keep doing it, the more it just normalizes it in society.

I was asked by a taxi driver recently if my girlfriend was my friend or my sister. It was none of his business but he asked anyway. I could have ignored it, but it was a direct question, so I gave him a direct answer: 'Neither. She's my lover!'

We were nearly at our destination, so I wasn't overly worried about getting thrown out. You do hear of awful hate crimes, so you do still have to be careful and judge each situation on its own merits. Even today.

So, if I had any advice around coming out, it would be don't rush it. Really assess the risks and make sure you're going to be okay. Only come out when you are good and ready. When you do, you'll find a whole host of organizations ready to help you. You'll also hopefully find some incredible LGBTQ+ friends. And enjoy it! Because I genuinely believe you'll be happier and more content when you can stop hiding who you are and live life as your true and wonderfully unique self.

'Every time I tell my coming out story I feel a little pang of guilt for how simple it was for me, because I know it isn't that way for everyone. Thankfully, the more coming out stories I hear, the more positive I feel – there is a whole lot of love out there – in all different places. Sometimes it's family, sometimes it's friends. But, just know, every time you look for it, this wonderful LGBTQ community will be waiting for you with its arms wide open.'

**Lucy Spraggan**, singer-songwriter

# Matt

'My whole family though that being gay meant you would move to London, get AIDS and die. They were terrified.'

Credit: Markus Bidaux and *Attitude*

*Author Matt Cain grew up in the 1980s and his parents were afraid of what being a gay man meant for their son's future.*

Well, I'm one of those people who is obviously different. I could never pass as straight. So, people used to tell me I was gay before I even knew what it was. It's really interesting, because when I was working at *Attitude* magazine, I remember us interviewing quite a few big stars who were very straight-acting men, and they were talking about how difficult it is to be gay and not realize it (because everybody assumes you're straight and you assume you're straight). I think there are challenges there. But for me, I had the very different difficulty of being one of those people who doesn't have the luxury of passing as straight. And therefore, you are thrust onto the front line whether you like it or not.

From the age of about five or six onwards, other people would remark on my girliness. They would say things like, 'He sounds like a girl, he runs like a girl, he talks like a girl. He's into girls' things. He plays with girls' things.'

I can say all this now with a smile on my face, without it being traumatic, because I've had a lot of therapy and I'm now 43. But it was horrendous at the time!

Of course, a girly boy is considered a freak, but a tomboy is considered really cool. There were always the standard jokes in the playground about limp wrists, and kids doing impressions of Larry Grayson and all that.

My era was a particularly difficult time to be gay because of the HIV/AIDS crisis. We were portrayed as dangerous, disease-carrying sexual predators who couldn't be trusted around children, and a lot of the taunts in the school playground reflected that: 'Don't touch him, you'll catch AIDS!' You know, all that kind of thing.

People talk about bullying now and they throw the word around willy-nilly when somebody just gets one negative experience with one person. There is a real difference between that and growing up in a world where universally you are told that the way you are is wrong. That you're a dirty, disgusting, deviant pervert. It's not just a bit of name-calling. I mean, some people do have a bit of name-calling and I know that is upsetting, but there's a difference between that and going out into the world and being met with universal loathing, fear and disgust. That marks you, and it marks the way you see yourself, and it shapes and determines your character and your behaviour.

So, I was forced to think about my sexuality before I probably would have done in different circumstances. I remember getting to an age where I realized that what the kids said about me was true. I realized what being gay meant. It wasn't dying of AIDS and wearing leather chaps, which is all we ever saw in the newspapers when it was Gay Pride once a year and *The Guardian* would cover it. I realized it just meant that you fancied men.

I came out before the internet, before social media, before mobile phones. You could keep a secret in those days. You could do it very gradually. I came out to friends at sixth form, and by modern standards this won't seem very young. Then I went away for a gap year in France, where I was looking after kids. Again, in those days people thought you couldn't be trusted around children, so I wouldn't say I went back into the closet, but I didn't come out any further.

By the time I came back to the UK and went to university, I was out to all my friends and exploring the gay scene. My sister came to visit me and I told her, then I told my brother, and then I told my mum and dad. By the time I told my mum and dad it was second year of university, so I would have been about 20.

My mum and dad are brilliant. But it's difficult to go over these things without being critical of people, especially when you work so hard on the journey together. My mum said she always knew, as mums often do, but my dad was very upset and didn't speak for a couple of days. The thing is, what I realized later, they were being conditioned by everything they heard about gay men. First of all, they thought it was a choice. Secondly, they thought that what happened when you were gay was that you disappeared into a London ghetto and you died of AIDS. They didn't have any examples of anything else. Basically, they wanted me to be happy but they assumed that being gay meant you were going to be unhappy.

It was a long process for them to come around to the idea. It was partly education from me, and at the same time the media was changing. Visibility was increasing, attitudes were changing, and antiretroviral drugs came in to treat HIV so that it stopped progressing to AIDS. Suddenly this panic started to lessen.

I remember thinking when my mum said that she always knew, 'Well, why didn't you say anything to make anything better?' and having a bit of low-level anger around that.

I remember a friend of mine was telling me that when he came out, his mum and dad reacted very badly and they said to him, 'This is really hard for us, you know! You've got to understand why it's really hard for us.' I felt really angry with his parents and thought, 'If you think it's difficult for you, how difficult do you think it is for him? If you think that all those bad things about gay people are true, he's heard them as well! How do you think he feels, believing that about himself?'

I can talk about all this now with a smile on my face, because I had all this therapy and I remember my psychotherapist saying to me, 'If parents recognize any signs of gayness, or otherness in their child, it's their responsibility to make them feel accepted and nurtured and okay about that, because anything short of nurture is abuse.' I mean, he was quite hard-line, but it's the parents' job to nurture their children and allow them to be happy as they are meant to be.

I've learned a lot about myself over the years. You change, you mature, and I feel wiser.

So many of us fear losing the love of our families and being rejected by them, and it was really important to me to give my family the chance to come on the journey with me and continue to be a major presence in my life. And I'm really pleased that I did.

If I could have a word in the ear of six-year-old me, I would say, 'Don't worry, it'll be alright. You have no idea how much better things will get and how different the world will be from the one you're living in now. Just hold your nerve, stick at it and you will be happy.'

I used to lie in bed at night, wishing I could flick a switch and not be gay anymore, or cut the poison out of me and all these awful things. It's my greatest blessing now. I just think it's like the best gift I was ever given. It's part of me and part of who I am.

The kid I was back in the day – clinging onto Madonna for dear life because everybody hated him – he would have no idea that my life would end up like this! I just wish I could tell him how much better things would get.

# Charli

**'People think if you're pansexual, you're in some sort of sex cult.'**

*Charli first came out as bisexual but now identifies as pansexual, which she says a lot of people don't understand. She is married but also in a polyamorous relationship.*

So, I got engaged to a guy when I was 16, but it was around the same time that I realized I wasn't straight. I was working at a loss-adjusters and they had a nurse who would go out and assess people as part of their insurance claim. She was a Geordie nurse and she was a tall, dark, lovely, gorgeous woman. She was really warm and open and that was the first time I physically had a crush on a real woman. I'd had crushes on people off the telly, but she made it become very real. I quickly realized that this was the same sort of stuff that I would feel about a bloke. I was still in a relationship, so I just started discussing it with my fiancé. I asked him how he would feel if I did something about my feelings. We'd often have these kinds of talks and he'd get quite turned on by the idea, so that would lead to a bit of fun. And that was kind of all that would happen with it. I'm not even sure if he realizes, but he was effectively the first person I came out to as bisexual. I used him as a sounding board really, to bounce ideas off.

The first person I came out to properly was my mum. She was just like, 'Yeah, we know. Okay. Alright.' I don't really know how she knew. She then spoke to my auntie, who was living with us for a while, and apparently she knew as well! I thought, 'Okay, so it's just me completely oblivious and everybody else knew!' My mum told my dad, which saved that conversation, but he was fine. We're not the best of friends but we understand each other a lot more than we used to. I told my sisters and my brother and they were like, 'Yeah, whatever.' And that was it! I was then open and out.

After that, things kind of got a little bit muddier. That previous relationship ended. I started working at the university in 2001 and I can remember meeting the guy who is now my husband on the first day. He let the door swing in my face, which he still doesn't remember! We then would meet up for cigarette breaks or lunch and have chats. We became friends. At the time I was seeing this girl called Sharon, who was 28, tall and blonde and beautiful. And I'd talk to him about her. I was just starting to finally explore that side of my sexuality. When I first started a relationship with *him*, we weren't serious at all. We just said we'd been friends, and now we were friends who were dating. We were friends with benefits! But fairly early on I said I'd still like to explore the other side of my sexuality. I asked, 'Can I still do that? Would you be okay with that? Would that be an issue?' He thought about it and actually said, 'No, it's okay.' This was 17 years ago.

I also told him that if he wanted to explore that side of his sexuality, I'd be happy for him to do that. He hasn't though and he doesn't want to. He knows that sexuality is quite fluid, so if things change and he wants to go that way, he can. I can't exactly say no, and I wouldn't! I would have no issue with him being with a man. A woman though...we would have to discuss it. Because that's what we do if something changes. Whether it's a job change or whatever, we would talk about it.

I'm so lucky. He's such a laid-back, chilled kind of guy. The interesting thing is that he only ever gets jealous of my friendships with men. He doesn't get jealous of me seeing other women. So, our polyamorous arrangement is that, yes, I'm married to him but I can have affairs with women. I've had a few affairs or shorter relationships, which have lasted a few months. We've maybe seen each other two or three times a month. It's not been an everyday thing. It tends to be with women who are in a similar situation – others who have the same sort of setup with their partner or husband. Long-term relationships with women would be different and I suspect that we'd have to talk about it. It's not happened.

I'm completely open about it with my husband, but if the woman that I'm seeing doesn't really want me to talk about what we do in the bedroom, then I won't say anything. But I would much rather be open and honest about all of it. We're open about it with our friends and families too. I know that some of my husband's mates don't like it and disagree with it. We've actually had discussions about it in the pub. I can completely understand it's not everybody's cup of tea. So, I've had to come out as being polyamorous as well. Being openly polyamorous makes sense – because if someone were to see me with a woman in some sort of steamy clinch or something, it could quite easily get back to my other half, and then that would put him in an awkward position. He'd have to go, 'It's okay – don't be offended for me!' So, I would much rather be open and prevent that awkward situation arising.

My mum always said to me that you can't judge anybody

else's relationship, because everybody's different. Everybody will have different nuances to their relationship. We're into BDSM [Bondage/Dominance/Sadism/Masochism]. We're not in the scene or anything like that, but we have our kinks and we are quite happy with them. You come across so many different people with so many different levels of kink. It's not just my choices; I'll defend almost anybody's choices, because if it's not hurting anybody (without permission), then just run with it if it floats your boat!

Coming out of the closet is not always an option for everybody and I completely understand that if you're concerned about your wellbeing; or if you are genuinely concerned about the impact it will have on your family, then that's fine. I actually have a relative who is gay. The entire family know that he's gay, but it's just never discussed. He never talked about it. We never talked about it. Not a word. And if that's what you prefer, if that's how you want to live, then that's totally up to you. Of course, I would prefer that everybody could just be able to be who they are and enjoy it, really. It would be a nice world if we could all do that. If we could just accept that everybody is different and everybody has kinks and everybody is a bit odd, then we'd be fine. It's the whole putting people in boxes and having them have to fit somebody else's ideal that I don't like.

I'll always get stick for being open about my sexuality and polyamory. I think it's the same thing as being a fat person. You get stick for being fat and you'll always get stick for being fat. I am one of the quote, unquote 'good' fatties, because I exercise and train a lot. But the stigma is the same because people have ideas of what you are because of the label. So, if you say you're a lesbian, people automatically picture in their head butch versus femme. They'll almost automatically have you either wearing a pair of Doc Martens or really glamming it up, whereas the majority of the time people are just people and they'll wear whatever they want. And it's the same sort of thing with people who are fat. People are fat for a myriad of reasons. Sometimes people are on steroids, which make you put on weight. Sometimes you are just fat. I have been a big girl since I was eight (or something like that) and have always been bullied because of my size. You get people coming up to you going, 'Oh, you're so fat!'

I've never been bullied about being bisexual but I have had a lot of questions and queries and people trying to understand and get their heads around it. And then we have the whole redefinition of bisexual versus pansexual. Actually, I think I probably am more pan than bi. The way I see it is if you're bi, you recognize that there are two genders and you're attracted to both, whereas if you're pansexual, you recognize that there are more than two genders. You can have gender non-binary, etc., etc., and all shades in-between and you're attracted to all of them. So, I just like people. It's down to the person and who I find attractive at that particular time. But it's just so much easier to say 'bisexual' because it's so much easier for people to understand. As soon as you start using the word 'pan' or 'pansexual', some people seem to think that you're offering some weird sex cult!

Then you've got the whole TERF [Trans Exclusionary Radical Feminist] element coming in now too. Those that don't believe in there being other genders. Those that don't even accept trans people. Why can't we just accept that people are people and there are lots of shades of people and lots of shades of gender and it doesn't matter?! There is beauty in diversity. It's such a nice thing to say. An even nicer thing to accept.

'We have one life and an amazing capacity to love and be loved. We must start by loving ourselves – that means accepting who we are completely. That's the first part of coming out; the second is recognizing that we must occupy our space in the world and not that loaned to us by being somebody else. Live. Love and be loved.'

**Michael Cashman**, politician

# GJ

## 'A newspaper outed me as a lesbian.'

*GJ struggled with coming out as a lesbian because of her Rastafarian faith. Her parents hail from Barbuda, near Antigua. She was outed without her knowledge by the* Caribbean Times *newspaper and had to make a tricky phone call to her parents.*

I just call myself a 'Black dyke'. I actually really like that. But yeah, I'm gay. I don't really like the word 'lesbian', I say 'gay'.

I think I've always been gay, because I remember trying to kiss my next-door neighbour when I was about eight or nine. I just thought it was normal. I just used to fancy my friends. I had boys as friends too, but I used to fancy girls. You know, I used to get those butterfly feelings. I didn't get that with the boys. I just want to play football with the boys or fight with them or just hang with them.

I grew up in Leicester in the 70s, and interestingly my dad used to have a lot of gay friends. My mum's uncle and aunt were openly gay too. It was quite different for that generation of Black people to be openly gay. My mum blames them for my sexuality, still to this day! My dad says, 'It's not from my side of the family – it's from yours.'

My parents are from an island called Barbuda. It's a very tiny island and when I go there everyone knows I'm gay and it's not a problem. They accept it, but I think that's because I don't make a big deal out of it. Like I say, my mum's uncle and aunt, everyone knew they were gay, but you didn't put the words 'lesbian' or 'gay' to it.

I remember getting to about 15 and all my mates fancying boys but I didn't. I actually ended up going out with a guy, not because I fancied him, but because everyone thought I was a lesbian and at that time I didn't think I was. I didn't know what name to give to some feelings that I had. I just thought everyone felt like that about their friends. So, I ended up going out with this guy. It didn't go too well because obviously I wasn't into men.

Then as chance would have it, I started working at a centre for women and girls, and then I met these two Black women that happened to be gay. I started to hang out with them and started to meet gay women, and then I kind of had a light-bulb moment. I was like, 'Wow! That's me!' I was around 19 at the time and I was a Rastafarian. I used to wrap my hair and wear African print. Obviously, within Rastafarianism being gay was seen as a sin, so I had real conflict within myself around my religion.

I ended up coming out by accident. I went on a protest march in London. I can't remember the cause now, but I was walking in front of a 'Black, Lesbian and Gay' banner and my picture got taken by someone from the *Caribbean Times*. In those days in Leicester, every Black person used to read the *Caribbean Times*. That was on the Saturday, and I think by the Wednesday word had got around about my picture...and oh my god!

I had one guy coming up to me and slamming the paper on the table, saying, 'What is the meaning of all this?' I said, 'Who are you? My father?' Everyone knew. I wasn't so much annoyed, I was more worried because I wasn't out. I was still coming to terms with my sexuality. I knew that my parents read the *Caribbean Times*, so I phoned them. I said, 'Guess what? I'm in the newspaper.' And they thought this was about my poetry, as I used to be quite well known around Leicester for my poetry. Then I said, 'But I happen to be walking in front of a "Black, Lesbian and Gay" banner.' And I remember my mum saying to me, 'Are you gay?' and I remember saying, 'No.' I wasn't ready. I wasn't ready.

I think they knew; they just didn't talk about it. It was a difficult time. I got a lot of hassle and I ended up cutting my locks and moving to London. Yeah, it was tough. I just got so much hassle. Mainly from women, funnily enough – straight women within my community. Moving to London was an eye-opener. I was like a kid in a sweet shop! It was mad. It was nice. I got myself a pair of Doc Martens, black Levi's, a denim jacket – you know that style back then? I grew my locks back, but more of a funky dread style, shaved at the sides. I could be gay and not feel worried about it.

Being outed was a blessing in disguise. I've always had a good relationship with my family, so I used to go back now and again. They kind of accepted it as long as I didn't rub it in their face. I don't know if that is them accepting it or not! I'd always take girlfriends home with me and they'd be fine with it, apart from when I took an obviously gay girlfriend home. I met an Irish lesbian in Lesbos, ended up having a relationship with her and took her home to Leicester. She was really butch and out and it was a problem for my dad, even though years ago he was good friends with a very butch lesbian. But she wasn't his daughter or her partner. I think even now my dad still has problems with me.

I've been out for 30 years now and I went away with my

mum last year. That was the first time my mum and I have had 'the conversation'. It was weird. And she said, 'We always knew you were a tomboy, but we didn't think you were gay until you brought that woman home.' My dad isn't ready yet for that conversation. Even after all this time, he's not ready. They know, so I don't want to push it on them.

I work with kids and I didn't come out at work. I didn't hide it or deny it, I just didn't put it out there. Then one of the parents invited me to her party, and a couple of the kids were nearby. One of them said, 'Why did his mum invite you to her party?' And I said, 'I don't know.' Then another kid said, 'It's because she fancies you!' And I'm like, 'Why would his mum fancy me?' And she said, 'Come on! We all know you're gay!' This is a 12-year-old kid! Kids nowadays are so astute.

To anyone considering coming out I would say, 'Just try and be as true to yourself as possible.' A lot of my anxieties were born out of fear and paranoia and not knowing. But you know, it's never as bad as you think it's going to be.

I don't have any anger towards the *Caribbean Times* – life's too short for that. Maybe it was a blessing in disguise because it helped me to come out. I've had 30 years as an out-and-proud Black dyke and met loads of lovely women because of it!

# Ellen

**'Being bisexual isn't the choice a lot of people perceive it to be.'**

*Radio producer Ellen talks frankly about coming out (or not!) and the challenges she faces, due to society's preconceptions about bisexuals.*

I kind of put it off, if I'm honest. I didn't come out at school, right up until I was 16. It was a very gradual process with my friends and then I guess you could say I've never really come out to my dad. Me and my dad have the kind of relationship where there are certain topics of conversation that just don't get discussed. I would never ask him about his relationships, and he doesn't ask me about mine. That's the understanding. With my mum, this is the most non-coming out story I think I've ever heard! I know I'm so lucky because other people have had such a tough time of it. Mine was just such a gradual process.

The first person I ever went out with was a girl and we started seeing each other when I was 15. We were both in school and we started hanging out and then kissing, and things kind of developed from there. She was hanging around at my house a lot and I was going around to her place a lot. One time we were making out in my bedroom and it got bit hot and heavy, so we were both quite flushed! It came to the time where her mum was picking her up. Mum walked past us as we came out of my room and as she was saying, 'Okay, lovely to see you...' she looked at both of us and said, 'Oh!' It was like she had clocked what was going on. We could see it on her face! We ran out to meet my girlfriend's mum and that was that.

I think my mum assumed that I was gay because me and my girlfriend saw each other for a year, but there was no conversation. The type of relationship that I have with my parents is very middle-class, stiff-upper-lip, 'Don't talk about it.' But then, paradoxically, my mum is a really accepting person. So, there was no big conversation and I feel like I was lucky in getting out of that because I'm quite a private person. That's the kind of thing that I don't really want to be talking about – not with my parents anyway.

My mum just accepted it and was perfect about it right from the beginning. She's met other girlfriends since. She assumed that I was a lesbian...and then I had a boyfriend. But again, there were no real conversations about it. I feel like I've cheated the system a little bit when I hear about other people and their coming-out stories that have either been embarrassing or awkward or had really awful consequences.

I didn't tell anyone at school though, even though I had a girlfriend. I didn't want to stick out. I didn't know anyone else like me. There were no role-models. I don't even think I knew what it meant myself. I knew it felt very natural to me. I knew how I felt but I didn't want to 'identify' and put my head above the parapet at school – I didn't want to be singled out as different. And I didn't know anyone else that I could have spoken to who was like me. But I've never been confused... I never remember feeling that. It's just something I never questioned.

The first person I fancied was a boy from New Kids on the Block, and he was quite effeminate! But when my girlfriend came along, it was so natural to me that I never questioned it. By 15 I knew that I liked boys *and* I liked girls and I could have a relationship with either. It felt very natural within me, but outwardly it was something I just did not want to share with friends at school because I didn't want to be different. Gradually they just found out over the years.

I think it's probably harder to come out as gay because parents perhaps think, 'Oh, well, that means I'm not going to have grandchildren', whereas I guess being bisexual, they might think there is still half a chance! Even though I don't really fancy having children myself, I think if I had actually been a lesbian, my mum would have probably talked to me about it at some point in a 'Does this mean I don't get grandchildren?' kind of a way.

I still think there aren't many bisexual role-models. We are really underrepresented out there! This might be controversial, but I really question some pop stars who have emerged onto the scene and use that label. I'm not sure whether they use it as a way to sell records or to be quirky and a little bit different and identify differently to other pop stars. But there are definitely some out there that have gone, 'Oh yes, I was bisexual but now I've just decided I'm only going to date boys.' So, it's really tough for bisexual people because that suggests you can make that choice. I don't think you can just switch off and say, 'I'm not going to fancy girls anymore, or I'm not going to fancy boys anymore.'

I think in the past the 'B' of LGBT has been a bit of an afterthought and sort of forgotten. I think it's getting better now and I do feel part of the community. I do like attending Pride. It's very much a part of me. I feel very strongly about it. And I feel very strongly that people should be able to identify as they want to identify and not suffer any consequences because of that in day-to-day life.

Yet there just aren't enough role-models out there. And the other trouble with being bisexual is the type of things that I hear from all kinds of people. For example, 'Oh I understand bisexuals, you just really love sex!' to which I always say, 'Probably no more than you!'

There is this idea that bisexual people are more sexual, that they get about a bit. I hear the phrase 'greedy' too. Things like that really upset me because there's such a misunderstanding of the fact that all being bisexual means is that I might have a relationship with a woman or a man. I'm not greedy. It really grinds my gears!

I would love to see a bisexual person properly represented in a mainstream soap like *EastEnders* or *Emmerdale*. Why not? We're just as valid and it would have been really valuable for me as a young person growing up, just to have that confirmation. Maybe had I had that I would have invested in coming out at school, telling more friends and having a support network instead of just bumbling along on my own. I can't emphasize that enough.

If you think you might be bisexual and maybe you're a little bit younger or you're in a situation that puts you in a vulnerable space, I would recommend you find a buddy that you can talk to. Whether that's on a helpline or in an LGBTQ+ group, try and find an ally. I wish I'd worked harder to find an ally, somebody to speak to about it a lot earlier. I think that's really important. Don't ever feel alone and don't ever feel like you're different.

'Remember, your sexuality and your coming out is no one's business but yours. There will be pressure from lots of places, but ultimately, it's nothing to do with anyone but you. You might want to be out, loud and proud, and that's cool, but you might want to keep it to just a small group or just yourself, and that's okay too. There's no rush. Give yourself a break.'

**Joe Lycett**, comedian and presenter

# Martin

**'I was at Stonewall.'**

*Martin Boyce was the son of Italian
immigrants and grew up in New York. He came out in the 60s at a
time when it was very dangerous to be gay in the city. He was at the
Stonewall Inn on 28 June 1969 and stood defiant, as the NYPD charged.*

I always knew.

In New York at that time, in the 1950s, people lived in the
same neighbourhood maybe for 50 years. The city was a collection of villages really, so to come out was very difficult because
everybody knew your parents, everybody knew your history.
Everybody knew everything from the moment you were born.

My father was a working-class man who drove a taxi. He also
trained boxers and he trained fighting dogs. When I was born,
he told me they all cheered in the bar because they thought
this guy is going to be a killer. Well, as it turned out, I may have
worn killer heels...!

My father had a cookie jar that he put bail money in. He
knew New York and he knew who I was hanging around with
and he thought they were bound to be trouble. He thought I

would get arrested. Amazingly, after two dozen incidents I was never arrested. People around me were – for vagrancy, loitering, disturbing the peace, whatever thing the police wanted to come up with. Especially with minorities. They were very, very tough on minorities.

What covered me, sadly, was the fact my mother was an invalid, so I was given a great deal of leeway in the neighbour-hood. Actually, the worst thing you could call anybody – even worse than a murderer – was a 'fag'. I mean, people that were released from prison had more prestige than fags. Even if they had murdered, they had much more prestige, because it was a butch world.

Coming out as gay just wasn't an option in the 50s. It meant isolation and a terrible, terrible life if you did it.

My sister had a very beautiful blue cape with a red lining. As my mother was in a wheelchair, one day they sent me to the store. Everybody had gone out except my mother, as she was in the chair, and I thought, 'Well, this is my chance.' I put the cape on! My mother could hardly speak but she tried to stop me. Nothing could prevent me. I went to Emma's, the Italian grocer, which was a wonderful place to go. She didn't say anything, she just looked at me. And I had my little pocketbook and I gave her the change for some pistachio nuts and some Sicilian salami. I will never forget it. By the time I got home the phone was ringing and it rang all day. The whole neighbourhood was calling! My father came home, and he said, 'Well, what's going on?' I said, 'I just wore the cape.' He said, 'Well, you can't wear the cape. It's a girl's cape.' I said, 'Well, I didn't know. I just wore the cape. I didn't have a jacket. I didn't know where it was.'

Well, my father, you know, he forgave me and the neighbour-hood calmed down and it was just another incident. But I knew. I learnt something, even if they didn't: never do that again, ever!

Keep it secret. Watch myself more, make sure my pinkie doesn't rise when I drink coffee. I made sure I looked at my fingernails the way a boy does, not a girl. I looked at the back of my foot the way a boy does, not a girl. Because I was being raised by straight people and I realized they were training me to live in their world. I might as well take advantage, and learn, and hide.

One time my father bought me a set of little iron Indians. I was happy until my sister opened her gift – a dolls' house! I collapsed! I cried for 48 hours in my bed, with my Sicilian grandmother, with her shawl and her gold earrings, staying over the bed and praying with her rosary. My father didn't know what to do! Eventually, he gave me some money and he said go to the store and buy anything I wanted. I bought a wagon and horses, and the wagon had a little spot where you could put this fake food. I took my sister's dolls' furniture, made a living room and a little kitchenette and put a string on it. I had a mobile home! That's when I remember my father saying, 'I give up!'

We then had an unspoken deal. I wouldn't make trouble, I wouldn't carry on and my father would go along with it. And he kept to that deal.

I had to come out one day, officially. What was the point of everybody knowing, if they didn't know? I decided in 1966, at the age of 16, that this was going to have to be announced! I told my father – he was great. Told my mother – she was great. Told my sister – she always knew.

I had to tell my grandmother – she was a *zingara* (like a gypsy). She was like something that came off a real old Italian olive oil can. You didn't want to puncture those kinds of cans and you didn't want to puncture her. She was a real old matriarch with her shawl, her gold earrings, her dark skin, her black hair. I said to her, 'Grandma, you know, you're the last person I have to tell that I'm a homosexual.' She said, 'Well what is that?' I said,

'Well, I'm gay.' She said, 'Well, why? What is that? Why not be?' I said, 'You don't understand. I'm a fairy.' She said, 'Oh! I told your mother when you were born. I told your mother you would be blessed. I told your mother you would never have trouble with women!'

I was very, very lucky. Drag queens would come to my house and they would put on shows for my invalid mother. They wore gardenias in their hair and were great, soulful singers. I just knew I wanted to be part of this great cultural endeavour, this great cultural world.

I remember going to Europe when I was a teenager. I went to Dachau, to the museum there, and the first time I saw the pink patch I couldn't believe it. I realized that this persecution of gay people wasn't just haphazard. This was systematic. The man near me said to his wife, 'Well, Hitler wasn't wrong about everything.' There was such sympathy for the killers and the haters. I couldn't believe what he said! From then on, I wanted to fight, and the only way that I could fight was to exaggerate myself, to force them to see me as a gay person.

I first met a crowd of other gay people in Central Park as a teenager. It was fascinating, exciting. It was a wooded area, so even my father couldn't find me with his cab! It was great. It was a great society in which I learned so many things, because all these queens knew something about culture or art or opera. But we didn't want to stay hiding in the bushes.

We would go to Macy's makeup counter and put on makeup. The security guards didn't know what to do! I couldn't believe a slash of crimson red lipstick could do this to them. They didn't know whether to call the police or try to speak to us. We used to gather together and go on outings like going to the zoo. Or we would go to the art museum, but no one looked at the art! There were about 14 of us, so it was very hard to attack us now. There was tremendous safety in numbers.

Gay people intrinsically know a great deal about survival – and if they don't, they learn quickly.

The Village was like nirvana. So many interesting people and we could be open. On the night of 28 June, 1969 I was going to the Stonewall Inn. It was the most popular bar in the gay city as it had dancing. They had a security man on the door and that night I ran into a friend of mine who said, 'You're not getting in, I was just there.' We were both in scare drag (it's sort of like Boy George, so not full drag) and they just didn't want any more scare drags in there. So, it was already near midnight and we decided, 'Well, let's plan what we're going to do', because the night was still young for us.

We were up the block from the Stonewall Inn on a stoop when we heard a commotion. Someone mentioned a raid and there was a crowd. We went to Stonewall, and the moment I got there, there was trouble.

There was a paddy wagon and a cop was pushing a drag queen in. I didn't see her, but I saw her shoe – it was like a famous Joan Crawford 'come fuck me' pump. It was jewels, it was straps, it was high-heeled. I never forgot it because I was mesmerized by that. She kicked him and pushed him back, and he got his revenge. He went back into the paddy wagon and you could hear bone against metal. He closed the door and he looked at us, as they always did, and said, 'Alright you faggots, now get the fuck out of here, you saw the show.'

Something happened. We didn't move. He was an ugly police officer and he had that horrible face that showed he knew what he was doing. He was arrogant and he enjoyed what he was doing even though it was routine for him. He just thought he could turn his back on us and that would be it.

But something happened. We did not move away, we took a step forward, all of us at once, without communicating. We took another step forward and another step. I could see the hairs rise on the back of his neck. He turned around to repeat the order, but there must have been a look on our faces. It was almost as if we were liberated from Dachau and now we had our oppressors under our control. There were so many of us. He gulped, he blinked, and the riot was on. All hell broke loose. Everybody had started throwing pennies, copper pennies. Anything we had (except anything valuable like our keys) we threw. The riot was just on.

All of this anger came out. All of a sudden, and without any precedent, leaders arose. The toughest drag queens took control. This one queen whom I admired was up on the Stonewall Inn window, egging us on with this firm face. I had never seen a face like that with such intensity. And don't forget, they were very poor queens.

The adrenaline and the need to react to this invasion was very important, and somehow we all realized that the most important thing was to keep it going. You see, we were always attacked – it was a city sport to attack gay people. We always knew how to regroup and get together again once we'd scattered. We did not know how much this would help us during the riot because we became very good urban guerrilla fighters.

The worst thing in a riot is silence, and the riot went silent. Not a peep, not a pin, but a hoofing sound, a storm trooper sound. And all of a sudden, the crowd parted and there was the tactical police patrol, armed to the teeth. I mean, I couldn't believe it. There was no part of their body that would be hit if you threw something. They were shielded, and they had every piece of equipment. They did not know what to do! They saw us, these queens, and we were in the middle because we were the best fighters, and they stood there, and we stood there. We didn't know what to do either. It was as if two alien people had just seen each other for the first time.

What we could do was form a kick line, like the Rockettes, and we sang one of our ditties: 'We are the village girls, we wear our hair in curls, we wear our dungarees above our nelly knees and when it comes to boys we really...' And that's as far as we got, because they charged. What could they do? They had to do something – it was too humiliating for them. It was the super butch facing the super femme. It was a world that was going to create a circle or fall apart.

Coming close to daylight, there was a change in the sky. It was over. I sat on the stoop exhausted. I looked across from me. There was this queen, sitting on the stoop, totally exhausted. Six feet away was a policeman, exhausted, no longer enemies, but never friends. As the sky lit up, all the debris, all the smashed glass, looked like diamonds catching the early part of the sun. It was one of the most beautiful sights.

Another gay veteran, Denny Garvin, said that after that we were a people. I think that's accurate. That's what really changed: our attitude changed. Even when I got home, my father said, 'It's about time you guys did something.'

But thank you to young people today for taking that torch and continuing. This is still just as much a fight as I had.

'Coming out is a bit like having anal sex for the first time. You dread it, but it's usually not half as painful as you thought it would be. It's all about being true to yourself. You're not living your life for others. But they will still love you. Courage, mes braves.'

**Iain Dale**, writer and broadcaster

# Sophie

**'We promised to never mention that we saw each other in a gay club.'**

*Sophie came out as gay at 17. Her mum really couldn't cope and threatened to divorce Sophie's dad. This, however, is a real story of eventual understanding and the realization that things do, nearly always, get better.*

I was about 15 and I was walking into town with my friends and there was a girl in front of us. She had a fairly short skirt on and she had really long legs, and I just turned around and said to my friends, 'Oh my god, that girl's legs are beautiful!' One of my friends then turned to me and said, 'Are you a lesbian or something?' And I said, 'Absolutely not!' It hadn't even crossed my mind!

Growing up, my dad always called me the 'lesbian daughter', as a joke, because I was never into boys. I was forever helping my granddad out with the DIY or the gardening. My nan and my mum, they'd go shopping and they would leave me with my granddad and I'd do all the DIY with him. So, I just assumed that I was a tomboy and I just never really thought about guys.

Then, around the age of 15 I started to realize that all my friends were into boy bands. They basically said to me, 'Oh, you've got to like one of them. Which one do you like?' And I said, 'I don't know.' So, they went, 'Oh, you can like this one. Here's your favourite!' And I said, 'Yeah, okay, cool.' So, it got to that point where I had to pretend that I was obsessed with Zayn from One Direction!

But secretly I had a closet door (it's even funnier that it was a closet door) in my bedroom with posters of Lady Gaga on it. My mum wouldn't let me have posters on the walls, so there's naked pictures of Lady Gaga still to this day on my old closet door at home.

It was just a weird time for me because I wasn't interested in guys. Then I went to sixth form and I became friends with a group of lesbians there. It still wasn't really clicking in my head though. I can look back now and see all these signs, but it still wasn't clicking.

I think what did make it click though, was this guy at my work that had a crush on me. He kept sending me messages and asking me out on dates, and I kept turning him down, saying I was too busy: 'I've got work, I've got school, I've got grades to get!' I finally accepted and I went out on a date with him.

We'd been dating for a little bit, and every time I met up with him I just started crying. He was like, 'What's wrong?' and I would say, 'Oh, I'm just really stressed. I've got a lot going on.' I think he just thought I was a really emotional female and simply needed hugs and attention. The more he hugged me, the less I wanted to be with him. I wouldn't tell anyone at work that we were dating. He asked if I was embarrassed about dating him and I would always say no. But I just really, really didn't want to be with him, so I broke up with him and apparently broke his heart in the process. I feel so sorry I did that. I was just so confused.

I did go out to a gay club at home in Kent with some of the lesbians I hung around with at school. I would sneak in, aged 17. I actually bumped into one of my teachers in there once. She tapped me on the shoulder, not realizing it was me, and started with the line 'Do you come here often?' I turned around and we both looked at each other and she said, 'If I buy you a drink, can we never talk of this again?'

The girls got me drunk once and asked me if I was a lesbian, and I said, 'Yes, but don't tell anyone!' I was still looking at guys at the same time, so I think I was trying to convince myself otherwise.

When I was looking at universities, I looked at Salford and I looked at Manchester and the Gay Village and it helped me make up my mind where to go. It was around that time that *Banana* and *Cucumber* had just come out on TV[1]. I'd seen the adverts, and my mum and dad kept joking about them. That was probably one of the main reasons I didn't come out so soon, but I put it on the planner to record. I came home from school one day and I heard my mum shout out to my dad, 'Why on Earth are you recording *Cucumber*?' He said it wasn't him, so she said, 'Who on Earth in this house is recording *Cucumber*?' I said it was me and she asked, 'Why on Earth are you watching this?' And the only thing I could come up with was that it was filmed in Manchester and I just wanted to see what Manchester looked like. My mum said, 'Oh, why don't you sit down and watch *Coronation Street* with me?' So, I had to sit through that!

Eventually I moved to university and I was in student halls. There were three boys and three girls in our flat, and two of the boys had a crush on me. I kind of went along with it as I was

1    *Cucumber* and *Banana* (and *Tofu*) were a TV series broadcast on Channel 4 in 2015. Created by Russell T Davies, the dramas explored aspects of LGBT life in 21st century Britain.

trying to convince myself that I was straight even though I'd known back home that I wasn't. It's incredibly strange. I guess it's what people say to you: 'Oh, you've just not found the right guy yet!' So, I think I was still just looking for that right guy, which apparently was going to turn out to be a girl! I just didn't know that yet.

I became friends with two boys on my course who were both gay and they took me out to the Gay Village one night. I had the most amazing time and I don't know what made me say it to them, but I just turned and said, 'I'm a lesbian!' From that day onwards I spent all my time with them and we used to go out to the Village. I got to know a lot of people there and had a close-knit group of friends that were all gay or lesbian. I would invite them back to my flat and my housemates would say, 'Who are all these people? They don't go to this uni. Why do you keep bringing them back?'

A few drag queens started to use the flat to get ready, and my housemates were just so in complete shock at the six-foot men in heels stomping around the flat that they started to hate it. So, I decided to tell them that I was a lesbian and they didn't react well at all. They were really rude to me and even threw some of my things out the window. So, I started hiding in my room a lot more or not coming home and going to friends' houses instead. We sorted it all out in the end and we all sort of became friends again. Towards that end of the year, I thought, 'Okay, so I've managed one battle of telling my housemates. I should probably start to tell other people now.'

I knew full well that my sister had an idea, because somebody had posted a picture of me kissing a girl. But I didn't know if anyone else in the family had seen that, so I held back and didn't say anything. One day I was on the phone to my parents on loudspeaker and my dad was just chatting to me about my life and stuff. I mentioned one of my friends and my dad said, 'Sarah is a lesbian isn't she?' And I said, 'Yeah.' And then he said, 'Are you a lesbian?' and I said, 'Er, maybe.' And he just started laughing! And I said, 'Is that going to be a problem?' And he said, 'Of course it's not a problem. Like absolutely not. You know, I love you no matter what. You're still Sophie to me!' All this time my mum was still there on the phone and she didn't say anything. I said, 'Alright, bye, love you both.' And my dad was like, 'Bye, love you', and he hung up. I had a huge sense of relief that I'd told them. I felt so happy.

I called my friend and I said, 'Guess what? I've just come out to my parents and they took it really well!' They said, 'Congratulations, we're so proud of you!' Then I hung up the phone and there was a message from my sister and it said, 'Mum is absolutely fuming with you. She's not happy that you're gay. She's shouting at me, asking if I knew anything about it.'

I'd come out a couple of days after my birthday and the day before my mum and dad's wedding anniversary. So, my mum then threatened to get a divorce from my dad on their wedding anniversary. I started crying. I didn't really know what to do, because in my head I'd always assumed that my mum would be the one that would be okay with it and my dad might have a bit of a problem. So, to find out that it was actually the other way around hit me really, really hard.

I tried to call my mum a few days later and I noticed she was blocking my calls. She finally replied to one of them and said, 'I don't accept this. I don't condone it. I don't believe in what you believe in.' At that point I just didn't know what to do. So, I called my dad and he said, 'I'm really sorry. I can't talk to you right now.' It turned out he was with my mum and she had said, 'Don't take that call.'

My dad called me later on and said, 'Your mum doesn't want

me talking to you anymore. So, if we talk, I'm going to have to delete all the calls and delete all the messages.' (She was going through his phone to see if he was talking to me.)

The only person I really had to relay information for me was my sister, because my mum obviously wasn't checking her phone or checking her messages. So, my sister was still able to talk to me.

This was all just before Christmas as well. So, then I had this hard battle of 'Do I go home for Christmas or not?' Being so young – just 18 or 19 – I thought, 'I need to go home for Christmas. I can't not go home.' It was the first time I'd seen my mum since coming out and my dad said to me, 'Don't mention it. If you don't say anything, it's fine.' So, my mum was okay with me until one evening. We were sat opposite each other on the sofa and I brought it up and it caused a massive argument. She was shouting, 'I don't believe in it. I don't know why you're like this. I didn't bring you up to be this way. I had dreams and aspirations for you. I wanted you to grow up and have a family of your own and get married.' And I said, 'Mum, I can still do all those things.' And she said, 'No, you can't! You'll never be able to get a job now. No one's going to accept your CV when they find out that you're gay! This is it, you're going to catch HIV now!' I kept telling her, 'Things have changed. This is not how these things work.' It was literally just a lack of education that was causing her to have such harsh views. It was difficult, though, because she just didn't understand it. She didn't want to hear any of it or didn't want to know, and it's hard to educate somebody that doesn't want to learn.

When my mum finally started to accept that I wasn't going to change, my dad actually told her, 'Oh yes, she might be bisexual.' He told me, 'If we give her a bit of hope, she'll take it slowly, it will ease her into this.' So, I think to this day my mum still thinks I'm bisexual.

A lot of the family still don't know because mum said, 'I don't want any of them knowing about Sophie.' But my dad tends to let things slip because he's proud that I'm a lesbian. He works with a lot of lesbians and he always introduces them to me. He said to me, 'It's so great that you've come out as a lesbian. It's like when you buy a new car and you start realizing that everyone around you has got the same car. I've been doing the same since you came out as a lesbian. All I keep seeing is lesbians around me!' So, he was so supportive.

It's better now with mum. I graduated this year and my mum, my dad, my sister and her boyfriend came up for my graduation. Afterwards we went for a meal and we decided to go for drinks where I work in the Gay Village. My dad went home after a while, but Mum got a little bit tipsy and I said, 'Why don't you stay out with us? I have never been for a drink with you!' So, she stayed out! I managed to get her to G-A-Y,[2] got her a few drinks and told her, 'Mum. I'm okay! I'm doing well. You can see I've got friends.' And she said, 'Yeah, I just want you to be happy.' I think that was the moment that we bonded. There's pictures of my mum over the years and she always does this half-smile whenever she has photos taken. There's a picture from that night of me, my mum and my sister in G-A-Y, and mum is smiling the biggest smile I've ever seen on her face.

That night, we went to another bar where my girlfriend was working, and she covered our drinks. Mum asked why she had paid and I told her that she was my girlfriend. I instantly thought, 'What have I done?' But Mum said, 'Okay, what's her name? How old is she?' and just was so accepting. She even went as far as to invite my girlfriend out for a meal the next day with

---

2    G-A-Y is a gay bar and nightclub located in Manchester's Gay Village. The original G-A-Y bar is located in Soho, London.

all of us to get to know her a bit better. So, I realized my mum might slowly be starting to understand.

Over the years, I've thought of so many different ways to come out. I thought of changing my bed into a massive big rainbow and explaining it that way, baking a cake...so many ideas. I'm sad that I didn't get to do it like that and that it was over the phone and I couldn't see my parents' reactions. Maybe things would have been slightly different if I'd seen their reactions, because I could have maybe talked it through a lot quicker with my mum, rather than having all those months of her ignoring me.

She still has her moments. When I broke up with my girlfriend, Mum turned around and said to my dad, 'I thought that might happen. She's definitely still a bisexual, isn't she?' So, baby steps, but we're getting there.

'When we come out, we could be changing the script our parents have written for us. Sometimes it's okay to give them some time. I did the total opposite: when my mum asked me to keep my voice down in case the neighbours heard, I screamed "I'M GAY" out of an open window.'

**James Barr**, comedian, actor, writer

# JJ

**'I fully expected to lose my wife when I came out. And I really loved her.'**

*JJ, or Jessie, is a gas fitter from Manchester who is happily married to a woman and has two children. But JJ identifies as non-binary or gender fluid and was terrified they would lose their family when they came out.*

I don't feel entirely male or entirely female any of the time. I would say I identify as a non-binary, gender fluid person. I'm just me. A person who just floats between the binaries as I please.

I think of gender as being an open playing field. There's a lot of people who are non-binary who will really rock a beard and wear a full face of makeup and a dress. I think everybody has their own style, but that's not really me.

Biologically, I was born male. I've obviously gone through male puberty, and I'm now essentially a grown male adult. But maybe in a different life, if I'd been aware of the stuff I know now, I may have transitioned as a young child and then now I'd be more feminine. But I still reckon I would be non-binary.

I'm 27, so no it's not too late to transition. But I don't want to go down that route now because I'm happy with the way things are.

I'm not offended if you call me by the pronouns 'he' or 'she', because I can present either way. I have friends out there who are specifically 'they' or 'them'. They do not want to identify as either female or male because they're strictly non-binary.

It's quite interesting that a lot of languages don't have gender in them. I think Turkish is one that has no 'he' or 'she'. There are no pronouns for gender. But for me, although a lot of my life has been male-dominated, I'm happy to go with 'he', 'she', 'they', 'them', anything.

I knew from an early age that I was different. My dad caught me dressing in my mum's clothes as a small child. I was probably three or four. That set me down a different path because his first reaction was to make a joke in front of everyone about it. As a child you then think it's wrong. I'm not allowed to do this. I shouldn't do that.

But dressing up just felt like something that I knew I had to try and experience. I was just drawn to it like I'm also drawn to playing football or watching boxing. No matter how far I went, I was always drawn to the feminine side of things as well as the masculine.

I did what a lot of LGBTQ+ people do and that's to run from who they are. I guess I spent a lifetime being the complete opposite to what I really was. It wasn't until the past couple of years that I decided, 'No, I'm a grown person, I'm an adult, I *can* face who I am!'

The trouble was, I had to come out to myself before I could come out to anyone else. It was still a battle for me because I thought, 'I'm not this person. I can't do that.' I was consumed by guilt and shame and fear of what other people thought. And then it just got to the point where I realized that I wasn't doing anything wrong, I wasn't hurting anybody, I was just being me and expressing myself!

I actually don't know the exact moment it sunk in, but I went to a fancy-dress party with friends, and I went as a female. I just knew at that moment that everything felt too good and I was probably happier on that night than I had been for a long time. After that, I realized I needed to have a hard talk with myself as well as with other people.

It was supposed to be fancy-dress but it was definitely more than that. I played the group idiot and joked about the fact that I enjoyed it too much! Really, I was in my element and I was thinking, 'Well, this feels different, but nice!'

I think my first night out as Jessie was about two years ago on Canal Street in the Gay Village in Manchester. And it was great, it felt amazing. I was meeting friends; we had a makeup artist meeting us and we'd gone for the full shazam. I was that scared, I thought I might end up staying in the hotel and not have the courage to go out.

I say 'friends' – they were new friends I'd met on social media who were going through similar stuff to me. When I joined social media, it gave me a whole new world of connection. It helped me come to terms with myself, because on social media people are themselves, even if nobody else knows about it. I know plenty of people who are closeted but they're themselves on social media.

After all those years of being scared of telling friends or family, Twitter and Instagram gave me a place to belong. I joined Twitter initially just to see if there were other people like me, and then it just opened up a whole new can of worms! I now have over 80,000 followers! The thing that I found was, it really gave me a place to belong. It's helped me become more confident. Also, through that platform I've had so many people message me and say things like, 'I'm married to a beautiful woman, I've got kids, I love them, but there's this side to me and I can't tell them. You've managed to do it. Can you help me do that?' It's been quite interesting seeing how many people want support.

That particular scenario is similar to my story. I'm happily married to a beautiful woman. I have two beautiful children and I have a really supportive, liberal family. My mum's great, my brothers are great. Everyone's been great really, but I think I was trapped in the prison of my own mind. For a long time, I had a fear of coming out to them.

So, I first came out to my wife. That was after the fancy-dress party, and at the time I was fully prepared to lose her. I didn't know how she would take it. You know, it's a big thing to say to somebody that you might be gender fluid. I didn't know what her reaction would be but I knew to go forward we had to be honest.

I didn't even know how to phrase it. I mean, I'd never even heard of terms like 'non-binary' or 'gender fluid' at the time. I just explained that when we did the fancy-dress party, it felt amazing. I explained that all my life I felt a little bit different. My heart was racing out of my chest. I didn't know how she'd take it, but to be fair she was amazing. She basically said, 'You're still you. I still love you for the person you are, so we'll go on this journey together.'

I stole her wardrobe and now she steals mine! She's just been an incredible rock. Even with coming out to other people, she's always been there. She's even offered to speak to people on my behalf. She's been great, because it's a big deal. Jessie is not really the person she first met, but she's gone with it. It took a lot of people by surprise because I'm not eccentric or camp or flamboyant. I'm a gas engineer, I ride a motorbike, I have stubble a lot of days.

To be honest, I'm still in the early stages of figuring out where

I need to be and where it's going to go. I'm just kind of keeping Jessie and JJ a little bit separate, just for now.

Recently, I had a former group of friends find out, and they didn't take it as well as some of my close friends did. But luckily, I've got so much love and support around me that those people who tried to mock me... It just backfired on them. So, I'm not too fussed about that.

My youngest child is two. She's an angel and she doesn't understand, so I'm not going to mention it to her yet. My eldest child is eight and I've had the chat with her. Before I properly came out to everyone, I did a photo shoot with a friend of mine. And he did some amazing photos of me as Jessie. I decided to show people like my mother-in-law and a few other people before they knew the full extent of it. I told them a bit of a white lie. I just made out I was helping a friend who had an upcoming business. So, we showed my eight-year-old girl a picture of me and she just said, 'Wow that's amazing!' Kids are innocent. They only know what they're taught. So, she was great. And then I had a proper chat with her and she was amazing. She just said, 'I don't care. As long as you're happy Daddy, it doesn't matter to me! It's fine.' Kids are just sponges: they soak in everything. And that's why it's important to have LGBTQ+ education at an early age – if we show them that it's okay to be yourself and express yourself, I think that'll help a lot of people.

My dad's quite difficult because he doesn't open up at the best of times. He just keeps everything to himself. It's not that we avoid the subject. I just think my dad needs to be in a place where he's okay to talk about it. I know he has no problems at all, but I'm still yet to have that conversation with him. On the other hand, I've spoken to my brothers and I've spoken to my mum. My mum's awesome. I introduced her to Jessie, and now we go out for coffees and she's really supportive. She encouraged me to come out to the rest of the family. There was no pressure, but she said I should go for it rather than let someone slip up or someone stumble across it or find out through other means. She came out with a brilliant quote. She said, 'Those that matter won't care, and those that care won't matter!' I just thought, 'She's right, really', and it was good advice.

It was great going out as Jessie for the first time. I felt like myself. I felt liberated and free for the first time to just be me. That gave me the confidence not to worry about what people think. I feel like everybody gets caught up worrying about what other people think about you. But actually, when you're out there, everyone's wrapped up in their own life and no one cares what you do. I have been out so many times now in the day as Jessie and no one bats an eyelid.

It's still something I'm learning about and growing with and I think I get a lot more confident every day. I have friends, for example, who identify as cross-dressers. They would say it's nothing to do with their gender identity as they don't feel like a woman on the inside. They just enjoy dressing up and that's that. I would see that more as being a transvestite and that's not for me. I've toyed with the idea of transitioning, I've toyed with the idea of hormones and blurring the two. I wouldn't describe myself as cis-gender anyway. If I *had* to fill out an official form and tick a box for gender, I would tick 'other' or 'MX'. This is a greater scale than just 'male' or 'female'. That's for sure. It's a wide spectrum. We all fit somewhere.

It took me a long time to realize that being both genders is okay. I didn't have to fix it. When I actually stumbled across the terms 'non-binary' and 'gender fluid', it really resonated. I finally thought, 'I don't have to make a choice to be this or that. I can just be me!'

My advice would just be: don't hide from it, come out to

yourself. Find out what you are, where you want to be and where you want to fit. And then once you've got everything that you need to know, then you can start sharing with other people.

I'm still on the journey, I'm still growing. I think there's a lot more to come.

I feel like now I've got a bit of a platform to do some good, so I want to do that. I'm confident enough in my own self to now be open and tell people who I am. Hopefully, that'll inspire a few other people to come out and tell people who they are, without being terrified.

'I have two pieces of advice that I can pass on from my experience of "coming out". The first and most important is: definitely don't be scared to accept who you are to yourself. Once you accept to yourself who you are, you've already made the biggest step! The second is: don't immediately demand understanding, just look for acceptance. Once your friends, family and co-workers accept who you are, the understanding will come.'

**Zach Sullivan**, ice hockey player

# Yvy

'When people noticed I was trans, I felt terrified of what they might do.'

*Yvy De Luca is the author of the memoir* Tainted Beauty. *She identifies as an Indian trans woman who is also pansexual. She really struggled to come out in the Muslim community of 1990s Blackburn and, for a while, led a double life.*

It was probably in my early teens that I had the idea or the feeling that I was female. I just didn't know how that was going to work out or how I could actually be that person. I remember at a very young age doing little things that, when I look back now, were such a massive giveaway. Things like putting jumpers on my head and pretending to have long hair. And always playing with my sister's toys and never using the toys that my mum actually bought for me. It's very common that we as trans people see those signs at an early age.

I grew up in Blackburn, which is a smallish, predominantly Asian town in Lancashire. It was the early 90s and people told me I shouldn't act in a certain way because I was acting like a

'Khusra' (a homophobic slur in Urdu), which means gay or poofta. I was being called gay slurs. That's what I grew up with. These days there's so much information at your fingertips, but back then I didn't know shit about anything when it came to LGBTQ+ people.

I didn't want to admit it, though, because I saw what was happening to me in the playground. I thought, 'If this is how people are treating me when they just think that I'm gay, imagine how they'd treat me if I actually said I *am* attracted to boys.' I didn't think I'd survive it, so I just kept quiet.

In Blackburn at that time I didn't know a single gay person, let alone a trans person. When I got to 18 and I'd just started college, I tried to immerse myself in gay culture. There was only one club in Blackburn and that was aptly named 'Never Neverland'. It wasn't necessarily a gay club but it had a gay night, and it was my only outlet really. I remember having to go to the club in disguise (wearing a big hoodie jacket) and not making eye contact with anyone. It had a big, steel, locked door and you had to knock on it and wave and say, 'Hi! I'm queer, let me in!' It was all a very 'cover of darkness' type thing. When I went there it was great because I got to experience gay culture and make a few friends. But once I actually saw how everyone was acting, I realized that no one was really thinking like me. No one wanted to be a woman. Nobody felt like a girl. They all just felt like gay men who wanted to be with other men. And that's when I realized that this wasn't for me. Obviously, I had some fun as well – of course!

As I got older, I realized that my sexuality is more that I am attracted to the person. I don't really care what vessel or what outer casing you have – if you have a personality that attracts me, I just gravitate towards you. And that includes men, women, anybody really. I'd probably define myself as being pansexual.

I just see myself as Yvy, and if I like you, I like you. If I don't, I don't.

I've had relationships with both men and women. I haven't had full, long-term relationships with women but I have had relationships. I think it's important to let people know that we shouldn't restrict ourselves and think that we have to fit a certain mould or a certain box. Just let yourself open up and be free and then you can start to really learn more about yourself. After I went through my transition, I started to realize that I could now explore my sexuality when it came to women. I wasn't ready when I was younger.

I came out probably when I was about 19 or 20 years old, and it was my mum that I told first. Then afterwards I told some of my friends. It was a really, really freeing moment because for years I didn't even know that 'transgender' was even a word. And then to have that light-bulb moment, that kind of epiphany – it was like everything that I'd gone through all made sense. I realized I could actually do something about it rather than just have it swirling around in my head, not knowing what to do with it. So, it was really, really great, and my mum was so supportive about it as well. I just told her that I feel like I am a girl and I now know that I can actually be a girl. I can actually be the girl that I know that I am. My mum just said, 'I knew you'd say something like this to me at some point. I was just waiting for you to say it!'

You see, I'd already come out to my mum as gay only a few years ago. Back then it was a case of trying to fit that mould. I just thought, well if I'm gay I must try and be gay or be the gayest I can be. But it just didn't fit. When I told her I was gay, the conversation was actually in a shopping centre in Preston! But instead of saying, 'Are you sure?', she actually said, 'So, when you were going to Oswaldtwistle all those times with that friend that we didn't know about, was that really a boyfriend?' And, yeah, it was! She really was more interested in where I was going and what I was doing than my sexuality. And that's kind of how it went with us. She's just great!

My mum was born in Tanzania in Africa and my dad is from India, but they both came into this country when they were in their early teens. My mum is the youngest of all her brothers and sisters, but she's come to be very open-minded and very tolerant and accepting of everyone. I think that's a really good attitude to have, especially given where she's come from and how she's been raised. I'm really blessed to have someone like her in my life.

In terms of my siblings, my sister pretty much said, 'Yeah, you just do your thing.' When I moved away, it wasn't a case of never speaking to them again. It was more a case of 'they're living their lives and I'm living mine'. With my brother it wasn't like we had this really tight bond anyway, so when I moved away, I didn't really see him for a very long time. But our relationship now is really good. As for my dad, it's really a non-issue because he was never really present. I just remember him being this person that lived with us and then he decided to leave.

Really the issues for me came from relatives and the Muslim community. I was raised in the Muslim religion. My whole family is Muslim, and Blackburn is very Muslim as well, so I was very much surrounded by people of this faith. It was extremely hard to be Asian, Muslim and queer. I didn't go to mosque or anything like that. My family went, but my mum taught me the ways of Islam and then gave me the choice as to whether I wanted to follow it or not.

The problems I encountered from the wider community were a daily thing. There wasn't a day that went by where I wasn't being told that how I am and how I'm acting and who I think I'm going to be is going to bring shame. I was constantly being told not to carry on as I was, or face being disowned. I even got that from my own GP! When I actually went to him and explained how I felt, he basically told me not to bring shame to my family. He advised me to hang out with my brother more, play football and do boys' things!

And that's kind of what I've grown up with. I saw it at school as well. The majority of the bullying came from other Asian people because they didn't like how I was acting. They basically made me think that who I am is wrong and that I shouldn't even exist because of who I am. My mum was heartbroken, but in the end I made the decision to leave Blackburn because I knew that I couldn't be trans and stay there.

I was leading a double life before I moved. I chose to transition at home and then travel to Manchester for work as a woman. I did it every single day without my brother or my sister even knowing that I was trans. The only person that knew what I was doing was my mum. I would wake up super early, apply basic foundation, put my outfit on, tuck and then put a massive, long bomber jacket on with a hood. I'd make it to the train station without any eye contact, get to my job, then go into the accessible toilets. I'd put together the rest of my outfit in there. I'd put in the chicken fillets, put on the heels and then go into work to do an eight-hour shift. Then I'd just do it in repeat backwards!

I did that for months while I saved up to move to Manchester – I couldn't wait. It was so hard, and sometimes when I was on the train, someone would clock me. These were among the most frightening moments of my life. It was so hard because I'm sitting there on a train with half my makeup on (because I couldn't take everything off) and trying my best to look manly, but it just didn't work. I went through all of that just so I could be me. It was so tough. And to be an Asian person as well – it's almost as if there's an added toughness, an added pressure.

I was playing a role. When I got to work, I had to act like I was this person that loved wearing four layers of foundation and eyeshadow and lipstick when really I'm not. I'm more a jeans and t-shirt girl with hair tied up and no makeup. But I couldn't do that because I had to cover up the five-o'clock shadow. So, I had to play that role as well.

Some people at work were okay about it and some were not. This was the early 2000s and we had the same issue that we're seeing now, which is people complaining that I'm using the women's toilets. I was actually assaulted at work. I did have some support from my manager, but then I was pulled in for a complaint that was made against me about using the wrong toilets. It's just one of those obstacles I had to work through. It's crazy because when you think about it, I'm just living my life. I'm not really bothering anybody, but apparently people have an issue.

I recently went back to Blackburn after not being back for years, and I saw things in such a positive way. I saw my family and it was so uplifting. And when I walked around town and saw all these things that I remember from my childhood, which were once quite negative, I was able to look at them and go, 'Wow! I learned so much from that experience.' I'm really glad that I'm in this state of mind now because it really shows that you can learn from every single thing that you've gone through and let go of it and then turn it into something positive.

I think it's important for me to be out and proud as a trans woman now, because for a long time I have been passing. I can walk down the street and no one really knows. No one clocks me and I think I've taken that kind of luxury for granted for many years. When I started my transition, that wasn't the case because there were tell-tale signs. And as the years went on, I started to get into the flow of just living my life. Just getting on with it. I felt I didn't really need to broadcast it to everyone. Then I started to think, 'Actually I'm taking that luxury of passing for granted and there are a lot of people out there who are going through the process, who maybe have been going through it for many, many years and still aren't able to pass in society.'

Having said that, we shouldn't be made to feel that that's what the goal is. We shouldn't have to pass for anything other than ourselves. And that's why I wanted to come out and be a really, really open and proud trans woman. I don't want people to think that you need to pass because you need to make other people comfortable. No! Just look like yourself and that's all that matters.

To anyone who's yet to come out I would say stay true to who you are because what you're feeling and what you know to be true inside you, as that authentic creation, is true and correct. So, go full force with it and don't be afraid because the people that are meant to stay in your life, they will stay in your life. You might be like me and you might lose your extended family relations but you'll keep the ones that are meant to be in your life, and that's all that matters. And even if you do lose family, there's going to be people who are going to be in your life who you can meet, like me, who can be your family, who can be your support.

You're not by yourself. And don't think that you need to conform to anybody. One thing my mum said to me is this: 'Don't ever think that you need to be someone else to please me. Because when I'm dead and gone, who the hell are you going to be pleasing?'

'Whilst there is no "right time" to come out, as soon as you do, you quickly realize that living in the closet is a half-life – the difference between living your life in black and white and full-blown colour. Just know that you're not alone and it's only by being true to and loving yourself that you can begin to change your life for the better.'

**Jen Brister**, comedian, actor, writer

# Enoch

**'They tried to get me to "pray the gay away".'**

*Enoch was subjected to conversion therapy and thrown out of his university for being gay.*

Hi, my name is Enoch Miller. I'm the officially unofficial Empress of West Hollywood. I'm a West Hollywood native. Well, I've been here nine years now.

I'm part Hispanic, so I know full well that the Latino community has a really hard time coming out because of Catholicism. It's never an easy choice, but, honestly, you'll never be happy in your life until you're honest with yourself and the people around you.

I knew I was gay between the ages of 13 to 15.

The first conversation I had about being gay was with a friend. It was actually terrifying because I was very afraid of my parents finding out. It was a conversation I couldn't avoid, though, because he knew I was gay and he knew that I knew that he knew. I just couldn't hide it. A lot more people were becoming aware of my sexuality. The joke was I was so gay that the walls knew!

This was in a high school in Texas. In that community you were labelled as either a steer or a queer. It's a very homophobic area. So much so that if you come out as gay, you sometimes fear for your life a little bit.

There was someone on my baseball team who suspected I was gay and I ended up having the whole baseball team chase me out of the field house with baseball bats. I had to lie my way through, saying it wasn't true. But from that day on I did my utmost to keep it under wraps. If I hadn't denied it, they would definitely have attacked me. In a place like Lubbock in Texas they are just not accommodating to LGBTQ+ individuals. It's not a small town, but it's a very small-minded town.

I kind of got outed to my parents by accident, thanks to MySpace, of all things! It was my senior year of high school, and a friend of mine put up some really explicit photos of me. I can't even remember what he wrote, but my parents saw it and questioned me about it. It was the last week of high school and I had to tell them that yes, I was actually gay. It was really daunting!

I couldn't really deny it though. They had enough proof, thanks to MySpace. My dad's a Southern Baptist pastor, so obviously it was a big no-no for me to come out as gay. My parents are very religious and even named me after one of only two people in the biblical world to be resurrected after death. And I'm the oldest of six as well. It's a very, very religious community, so it was not a good idea for me to come out. But they did find out and then they immediately started talking about where to send me to get me fixed. I actually did conversion therapy. I was sent to straight camp for a little bit in 2007 to 'pray the gay away'.

I don't think it was nearly as bad as some of the things my other friends have experienced. I had friends who were part of the Mormon Church. They were a little bit more extreme. Some of them had ice-bath therapy or electroshock therapy – you know, the kind of stuff they did to prisoners back in the day. Cold-water therapy is part of the deprivation therapy that they do to mentally correct you. It's an old practice they used to do in insane asylums to correct mental illness. And honestly, I've come across a lot of people who still believe that being gay is a mental illness.

A lot of people don't realize there are these places called 'black sites' in the Southern United States – places where they send you and no one really cares what happens to you because you're going there to be fixed, because, apparently, being gay means there's something wrong with you! It's not a regular thing and it doesn't happen all the time. But you do get those instances where families almost think you're unclean, so they're trying to do everything they can to correct you.

My conversion therapy was more subdued. I had a lot of people laying their hands on me and praying. All I did was just lie through my teeth and tell them what they wanted to hear. I did that so I didn't have to deal with it anymore. I just wanted to move on with my life!

And then several years later, when I was 22, I met my partner, Doug, who I'm with now. I've been with him nine years now. At the time, I was going to a Christian College, which found out through Facebook that I was dating him. They confronted me and ended up expelling me from college for it. So, I also got kicked out of university for being gay!

Up until then I was trying to do what my parents wanted. Trying to fly under the radar and not really admitting even to myself who I really was. But when I met Doug I realized I couldn't deny the fact that this was the man I wanted to be with for the rest of my life.

I just couldn't be on board with pretending to be someone

I wasn't, so I finally officially announced, 'Hey – I'm gay!' From that moment onwards I basically said, 'If you don't like it, I'm sorry. That's kind of how it has to be!'

And because of that my parents then disowned me. It was hard. In fact, it took me about three years to really understand it and process it. The last thing I said to my parents was, 'This is what *you* want to do. This is *your* choice. I know who I am. I know what I am. And no matter what you think or say, I know that this is who I am.'

I also left it up to them if they wanted to make contact. I said, 'I'm always here if you want to talk. My door is always open until the moment you're ready to do that. I'll wait.'

So, the ball's definitely in their court if they ever want to talk to me again. But that was nine years ago now and they still haven't picked up the phone and called me. I don't think they ever will now.

For the first year or so it was really tough. As I said, I'm the oldest of six. So, when all that family, all those people you've grown up with your whole life turn their backs on you, it's kind of like a slap in the face!

I did try and talk to my brothers and sisters. I have one brother that still talks to me. I'm actually seeing him at the end of this year with his family. You take your victories where you can get them! The other ones have an ulterior motive. They talk to me but mainly just so they can tell me that I need to find Jesus. And I don't really have time for that. I mean, if they're not going to be uplifting to me and actually care about me and my future, then I don't want the negativity in my life.

But then I realized I have a new family. I have my partner, my sisters-in-law, and then I have every friend I've made here in West Hollywood. They're my surrogate family and they're the ones that love and support me unconditionally. They're the ones who I appreciate the most.

Especially here in West Hollywood, but also in Los Angeles, I feel we have to find the people to become our own families. LA, as progressive as it is, has about 8,000 homeless LGBTQ+ youths – kids that are kicked out for one reason or another or shunned by their families. It's not uncommon at all. So, I just want people to know that no matter who you are or where you come from, you will always have a family here with people that love and respect you and can understand you.

I know my story sounds quite depressing – but do you know what? I have no regrets at all about coming out. Honestly, I was more miserable lying to myself and lying to everyone else. Pretending to be someone that I knew I wasn't was so hard to do. Obviously, it wasn't an easy choice; but quite frankly, the moment I started being myself and really admitting to myself that there was nothing wrong with me, that I was beautiful and this is who I was meant to be, that was the moment my life got a whole lot easier.

My life wasn't an overnight success, but I've got all I have now by being around people that supported me, embraced my craziness, in whatever form that may be, and just really loved me unconditionally.

If you do come out, you'll be pleasantly surprised by the people that come forward and support you – people who you would never in a million years have thought would care. And those are the people that really will be your family from now on.

# Bill

**'He told me being gay was nothing to be ashamed of.'**

*Bill grew up in a care home for children in Southport and came out as a young man after being bullied. He went on to have a successful career, working in modelling and fashion.*

I was about 13 years old and at an all-boys school in Southport, which is where I was brought up (I lived in a care home run by Dr Barnardo's for 17 years). At that age I didn't know that I was gay or what the word 'gay' even meant, but I became very attracted to another boy a couple of years older than me. We formed a friendship. It wasn't sexual, but I just knew that I was absolutely, passionately and madly in love with this person.

Some of the other boys noticed that there was something quite strange, in their eyes, about this friendship. I used to go over to my friend's house all the time and I got to know his family. We went out together at weekends and I went on holiday with them. By the time I was about 18 years of age, snide remarks were being made about me, using terms like 'queer', 'shirt lifter', 'bum boy'. And for me, because I'd heard those words with negative connotations, it was actually quite frightening.

It got to the point where, on one particular day, I couldn't cope with it or deal with it and so I just decided to run away from school. I was away for about six or seven hours – over in Victoria Park, which is near where I lived. I eventually went to my Boys' Brigade and found my captain and explained to him what had happened. I talked to him and his wife and they then took me over to see my reverend. He was an incredible man. They got in touch with the children's home and the man who ran the home came and they had a discussion. I was not in that meeting, but afterwards I was asked a particular question. Looking back now as a 60-year-old man, it was amazing how it happened. They asked me if I was – and they used this term – 'a homosexual'. And then the reverend said that this was quite normal for a boy of my age. He told me that we go through these changes and that I needn't define myself as a homosexual at that point in life. Then he added that if I am, then I am, and there's nothing to be ashamed of.

That was way back in the 70s, so it was an amazing response – especially from someone in the Church. The head of the school, who was a good man, was informed and he thought that the best thing that could happen was for me to discuss things with some of the other boys. And so I did.

I did have a little bit of negativity, but most people actually just didn't bat an eyelid. It wasn't even discussed. I was quite athletic at school and I was very popular, so that certainly helped. I was fun and I was always able to get people laughing, so in the end the negativity dissipated quite naturally. But once I'd made that decision and I knew what I was, I didn't hide it.

I remember the first relationship I had was when I was around about 16 years of age. And by the time I was 17, I was popping down to London.

But to go back to the original guy that I fell in love with at the age of 13, I never even told him about my feelings. I think he knew and I think that's why our relationship changed. He sort of withdrew and moved on to other people more his own age. I didn't tell him at the time, because I feared rejection. It was a pivotal moment though. He was the first love of my life and I still find even today that if I meet people with the same temperament or similar looks to him, I'm attracted to them. I did look him up years later and he went into the Royal Air Force and he's now married with kids.

When I came out in the care home, a couple of the older boys didn't like it. It was a difficult time. The home was closed down because of sexual abuse. It was the children that had it closed down, because we all ran away one day. I was one of the older ones who helped organize it. Can you imagine the amount of social workers running around between Southport and Liverpool trying to find us? In the end Barnardo's closed the home down. They did the right thing. They investigated it and the person who ran the home was removed. It was a bad time and a sad time. If you take all that out of the equation, I have to say the home taught us a lot of valuable things in terms of our education, our manners and our development.

Sometime after that I moved to Manchester. I went to a club called DeVilles, which was very much an underground club. People like Morrissey and The Smiths would be there, and there were different styles, different fashions and different types of music from northern soul to funk to disco to what we call indie music today. And I just found this group of people that were mixed up with it all that were both gay and straight and it became a real culture. I then discovered other bars and that took me into the gay scene. I worked in the city centre and I was well known, so I never had any problems, like some did, getting into bars and clubs.

I've honestly never had any problems being out, gay and Black. I think anybody who knows me will tell you that I will automatically defend myself in front of people if I feel that there's anything that's based around race. If anything's said, I'm straight on it and I challenge people. However, I also understand that it is difficult for a lot of the Black youths to come out because of what's going on within their own communities. It can be extremely frightening for them. I've met individuals who've told me about their experiences and it's not something that anybody would want to go through. So, you know, coming out is different for all people. Other people of my generation had horrendous times coming out. I'm just one of those very lucky stories. I was very lucky with what I had around me.

I told my mother later on in life. I'd been out to a club and I'd got drunk. She was in her bed reading a book and I was sat on the edge of the bed and I kept saying, 'Mum, I've got something to tell you!' and she was going, 'What is it?' And I said, 'Well, I can't tell you', and it just went on and on like that. She eventually said, 'For god's sake what is it?' In the end I couldn't say the full word. I spelt it. I went 'I'm G...A...Y.' And she just said, 'Oh, never mind. Go to bed. We'll talk about it in the morning.'

And of course, we didn't really talk about it in the morning. It didn't need to be discussed. I think the only thing that she was concerned about was that I didn't bring anybody home with me. I don't think that was because of anything bad, it was because I had younger siblings. I think she just didn't want me to expose them to that. I understood that was more about respecting being at home. She's never had an issue with me and my sexuality. She's 85 now and she lives with me in my house, so that should tell people a lot.

I adore my family and I've been very, very lucky because they've been open and very accepting. All my nephews and nieces have had that experience of having me as an uncle and so their attitude towards the LGBTQ+ community is absolutely open. They've done the gay bars and clubs, they've got gay friends, and I love that. It is about normalization and that to me was very, very important.

Considering I grew up in a home, I've gone on to have a pretty amazing career. I've modelled for C&A and M&S. I trained in theatre (originally at the Arden School of Theatre), then I did a post-grad in playwriting. I didn't know whether I wanted to be an actor, but in the end I used what I learnt in theatre school and I went on to train models. I went on to develop models for one of Manchester's top agencies and I still produce fashion shows. In the 90s I did international shows. But I've done loads in my career. I worked for British Airways as a flight attendant, I've had my own business, I've run clubs, I've DJ'd. I'll do anything!

I think for me it's been relatively easy coming out, but I know for others in the Afro-Caribbean community it is very, very difficult. In my experience, a lot of people in the community find it very hard to discuss LGBTQ+ issues. I think that's because the community is very entrenched in Church, the old Church. In particular, young Black males living in cities in the UK get involved in this whole brotherhood thing. I would love to see older gay Black men mentoring young Black gay men, because they need that guidance. They need that help, and in some cases it might be that they haven't had a strong male role-model in their life. Particularly one that's gay. They might need that help and that foundation, something that they can cling on to.

I sometimes worry about the ageism in our community, though, because there are a lot of older gay men that are quite isolated. I'd like to see something done to keep a bridge between the young and the older community. The way the scene or the business side of it sees older men isn't great. We become irrelevant at times, unless you've got money.

In terms of advice, I think knowing who to come out to is really, really important. I think that's the first thing. I think you need somebody that you absolutely trust, somebody that you can confide in and then use that as your platform. But I think you also need to look at your outer network as well. Because you do get the horror stories where the family literally throw that person out and they've got no support. I've met people where that's happened, and they can't rely on their family at all.

So, then it becomes a case of creating what will be your family. Your family will be the LGBTQ+ community. That's where you're going to find that firm family that you need.

'Loneliness and isolation are huge problems for LGBTQ+ people, especially before coming out. Don't stay stuck in your head: reach out to people, anonymously or publicly, but don't isolate yourself. Outside of your own thoughts and fears there are people like you who all had to go through a similar decision and initial leap, and they'll be able to help you find your courage and eventually your people.'

**Bright Light Bright Light**, singer-songwriter

# Kerry

'I was into my 30s before I realized
I was a lesbian.'

*Performer and comedian Kerry Leigh was in heterosexual relationships
her whole life before realizing she was gay. How did her friends and
family react?*

I didn't actually realize I was gay until I was in my mid-30s.

I'd been in a relationship with a man for ten years and we had
two children, and then a light bulb kind of went on.

I totally wasn't expecting it. There wasn't a lead-up to it, but
when it did happen a lot of things made sense. For example,
I always remember there was a beautiful girl in my first year
of university and whenever she walked into a room, I couldn't
speak! I used to laugh about it with a friend. It didn't occur to
me that I was gay and I kept going out with men.

I didn't feel like I'd been living a double life or anything, but
what happened is the person I ended up marrying (who I am
sadly no longer with) became single and I started following her
around. Literally! And I didn't understand why. I was just really
drawn to her and kept making sure I was where she was.

So, it was one person that I fell in love with and she always used to joke, 'You're not gay, you just love me because I'm amazing!' But I just am. I just know that I am.

I don't even identify as bisexual, despite having had a long relationship with a man. And I've been challenged on this a couple of times by one person in particular: a gay man. He won't have it and says, 'No – you *are* bisexual!' But I think that's kind of for me to say and not him! I just am, it's just a feeling.

When I was first with a woman, it was like coming home. That's the best way I can put it. It just made sense. I thought, 'Why didn't I work this out sooner?!'

Do I regret that it took me so long? I've thought about that quite a bit and I don't think the word is 'regret'. I think if I'm truly honest, I probably would have liked to fuck a lot more women, because I would have done in my 20s and 30s!

But the relationship with the father of my children produced two amazing little girls and I could never ever regret that.

Coming out in my 30s – and I get emotional talking about this – was so easy. And I think that's because so many others have paved the way before me, so I haven't had any crap at all.

My parents aren't together, so I told them separately. When I told my dad, he broke into a massive smile and got a glass of whiskey, and he was happy. He was so happy! I think because he's just happy to see me happy.

For Mum, it was more difficult, and not because of any homophobia – it was literally a physical distance as she lived in Australia. Telling someone over the phone is different; it just is. And she struggled with it. I just said, 'I've met someone and that someone is a woman.' And I think the line went quiet for a bit.

She didn't struggle with it in the sense that she was being negative. She was just like, 'What? What?!'

She thought it was just a phase but she had only ever known

me to be with men. What she said – and it was so moving – was this: 'It's just really hard knowing that you're closer to another woman than me.'

So, when I fell in love with a woman, I think my mum was heartbroken, if that makes sense, because then I was closer to someone else who was a woman. We'd always bonded over crap relationships with men, to be fair. Then she met my wife and fell in love with her as much as I did, and it was all good.

I have actually spoken to people about this. It sounds a bit daft, but I almost feel guilty that I didn't have much of a struggle, because I know so many people did. I just feel I'm very fortunate.

When I came out at work, it was the funniest coming out ever because I'm quite an attention seeker! I was hosting my regular comedy night and I walked out on stage to the song 'I'm Coming Out!'

And nobody cared. Nobody cared! They were just like, 'Tell us some jokes, we're not really interested.' I remember telling one close friend, who said, 'Kerry, I worked it out years ago. Why has it taken you so long?' So, I was just like, 'Where's my moment? I want my moment!' and no one gave a shit!

Coming out is a very, very individual journey, I couldn't advise anyone that 'this is the way you should do it'. I would say choose carefully who you come out to initially. If you feel that there's someone that's going to be resistant, then initially come out to someone you feel safe with.

I'm not sure there is a right or a wrong way, but I suppose the only advice I would give is, because we do this with anything we're a bit frightened of, we drag out the build-up and that's not good for anyone. So, just crack on!

# Chris

**'I want to become Ireland's first gay strongman.'**

*The first relationship Chris McNaghten (or Chris Bear Strong as he is known in the strongman world) had ended up with him being blackmailed. He talks frankly about his struggles with mental health and tackling homophobia in his sport head on.*

I'm 30 years old now and I remember right back at 12 or 13 having a lot of confusing thoughts. I grew up just outside Belfast and there was nobody at that time I knew who was gay. There were only ever negative conversations about gay people who were on TV and I suppose that is the main reason why a lot of people didn't come out. If people got suspicious that someone was gay, that person just got picked on – the normal homophobic hatred. It didn't feel like an option to come out. The lifestyle in Northern Ireland at that time meant it didn't even feel like an option to explore being gay. As I got older, the feelings got a lot stronger and the confusion got a lot stronger too. I suppose I was lucky as I was attracted to girls too, so I did go out with girls until I was 28. I felt I was bisexual until then, but the reason I came out as gay was because I realized eventually that I really only wanted to be with guys. So, I needed to face my fears and come out.

When I was 27, I had a relationship with a guy. Anyone who knew us, knew us as mates and it was kept dead secret for over a year. Some people were suspicious. A best friend at the time knew and we had a couple of very close friends that knew, but that was it. To everyone else we were just mates.

I remember we went down to the very south of Ireland for a weekend away and we actually thought we'd act like a couple publicly, to see what it was like. It was exciting to hold hands in public and to show affection to another guy in public for the first time ever. But then there was that security blanket: nobody that knew me was going to see me down there, so I knew I was in a safe zone.

The relationship I had with this guy came to an end because things got more and more complicated. I hadn't tackled my fears yet. Some people I knew suspected we were more than mates and threatened me. Within my business life, there was a conflict of interest, and this person said, 'Tell me this, does your dad know you're gay yet, Chris?' It was thrown in my face. He was basically saying, 'If you don't do this, I'll let people know you're gay.' That caused a lot of stress on the relationship and the relationship definitely came to an end because we weren't open and we weren't honest. It ended up ruining the relationship.

So, a few months later, I sat down and thought, 'Right, what direction do you want to go in?' I just knew that I wanted to fully explore going into relationships with guys and being gay. I thought, for the first time in my life, that not being out was actually holding me back. So, I needed to face my fears.

I'd got a bigger public profile and I thought that as long as my family and close friends were okay with it, that was all that mattered. If they could accept my being gay and come to terms with it, nobody else mattered. If you sat and worried about the opinions of everybody, you'd never ever achieve anything in life. Every step I've made in business, every step I've made in sport, every step I've made that has been a success would never ever have happened if I'd worried about the thoughts of everybody around me. I looked at the people who were closest to me and I was like, 'I'm going to tell them.'

Friends-wise, I did lose a few. I guess that a lot of your normal banter, craic, in a close friendship, once you're revealed as gay, a lot of guy friends don't like that anymore. There was one guy and we were having some banter and I went to do a rugby tackle and he jumped back. He had never done that before, and it was clear that now that I was gay he didn't want to be that close to me anymore. Another really good friend always hugged me when we saw each other but since I came out, he never wanted to touch me. That was a wake-up call. So, I did lose a few friends, but I gained a lot of brilliant friends in return.

Family-wise, the family had to adjust. I was 28 years old and they had known me my whole life as being in relationships with girls. It was a shock and it was a surprise. I told my mum first. I said, 'You know the relationship with me and such and such? There was more to it than just friendship.' I think my family had their suspicions and my mum just said, 'We'll get through it, we will work it out.' It came as a shock to my family and you can't expect parents and friends and family to just throw their arms open and hug and say, 'This is amazing, this is brilliant', because it's an adjustment for them. They need to be able to have time to get their heads around it.

The one I struggled with the most was telling my dad. That was the scariest bit. I told my mum and she was getting very stressed that she knew and Dad didn't, and then she actually told Dad for me. It took about three or four days for him to get his head around it. Things were adjusting and things were changing. I ran my own business and the minute I told a few people, everybody started to hear straightaway. It was typical of where I am from and it was getting really stressful. I'd had a rough day and Dad still hadn't spoken to me. I got home from work and Dad came into my bedroom and came and kissed me on the head and said, 'I will always love you, no matter what', and walked out. And that was all the conversation we had and that was all I needed to hear at the time. I just thought, 'Fuck you' to anybody else. As long as I have my dad and as long as I have my mum, my sisters, my close friends, nobody else matters.

I can't tell you how lucky I am to have a family. Not everybody has that sort of love and that sort of acceptance. It was a huge thing for my dad to accept, and he needed to take time to get his head around it. You need to give people time and space. You need to help people to understand it, because as soon as you tell somebody, they're going to have a million questions (especially when you're from Northern Ireland, you know, because these lifestyles aren't seen publicly in Northern Ireland). My parents had a lot of questions: 'Have you always been this way?', 'Did you go out with girls just to keep us happy?', 'How long have you been struggling?', 'Is this why you had mental health problems?', 'Is this why you've been unhappy at times?', 'Why didn't you tell us sooner?' So many questions that they needed to have answers to, so they could get their heads around it.

I know one of the issues around my mental health was the self-loathing I suffered about my body image. I was bullied at school for being overweight, and then the type of guys I was attracted to isn't the way I look. I think this is where a lot of body image problems with LGBTQ+ people come from. We may be attracted to the same sex, but a lot of us are attracted to people who look different to us. I always saw the guys I was attracted to as having a good-looking physique. That is the attractive way to look and the way I look is not attractive at all. So, I beat myself up over it.

I couldn't accept that I was attractive, because what I found attractive wasn't the way I looked. I couldn't get my head around that. I couldn't understand why people would fancy me, when I wouldn't fancy me.

Part of my recovery was working on my body and becoming a strongman. But strongman definitely disguised a lot of it for me because now I had this sport that allowed me to be big. I had a bit of a label. This is why I'm big, this is why I'm this size, this is why I carry a bit of extra body fat – it's because I'm a strongman. Honestly, I can say it's only been I the last two years that I have been 100 per cent comfortable in my body and proud. If you saw my Instagram now, you wouldn't ever think I had a problem!

When I was coming out, it was never going to stay low-key, it was going to be a big thing. Because of my sport, I just had to own it. As soon as I came out and I put myself out there, all these messages started flooding in, with people saying how they found me attractive. At the start, it was hard to accept that; I didn't know how to take it. But hearing all that for the first time, that's what gave me the confidence to start loving myself again. I was able to see myself in a different light. I can see that my type of body isn't what I'm attracted to, but there's people out there who are.

There have been some instances of homophobia within the strongman community, but only from a small group of people. But when I was trying to compete in *Giants Live* (the biggest live strongman show in the world), that was a totally different ballgame altogether. There's another strongman who's openly gay: Rob Kearney, from America. *Giants Live* told his story on the strongman TV show, which shows just how accepting they are.

Generally, in the strongman world everybody is so supportive and so okay with being gay and there's only a very small amount of people who would cause any problems.

I'm out now, I've got nothing to hide and I'm ready to compete in 'Ireland's Strongest Man' and win as a gay man. I want to do it for myself, but also for the LGBTQ+ community in Northern Ireland.

'I'd say to anyone coming out, pick who you initially confide in. You'll know who's the right person, you'll feel it. And before you go to your parents to tell them, have that person on standby. When you come out, you're dealing with it too. You can't be expected to make everyone else okay with it initially as you're dealing with it yourself. And that's okay. It's okay to take some time for you. Anyone who's not okay is not worth holding onto.'

**Heather Peace**, actor, singer-songwriter

# Kate

**'Growing up Catholic, I wondered if god would be okay with me being gay.'**

*Kate McCabe is a stand-up comedian. She grew up in Pennsylvania but then went to university in New York City, where despite having a gay best friend, you will never believe who she chose to come out to first...*

I think it's interesting... Sometimes as a lesbian or a gay person, or somebody who identifies somewhere else on the sexuality spectrum, you might get asked the question 'When did you know you were gay?' But that's different to 'When did you feel different?' I remember feeling, in a non-sexualized way, drawn to women very early on. Like when I was about six years old, I had little tiny crushes on female teachers.

I started feeling different to other girls around 12 or 13 when we started going through puberty. All the other girls were gravitating towards boys, trying to get their attention and flirting with them. But while my female friends were all picking their favourite members of New Kids on the Block, I was scrambling to make up some random attraction to one of them!

I grew up in Erie, Pennsylvania, which is on the Great Lakes in America. I wouldn't call Erie a hyper-progressive city; I would describe it as very Americana. It's traditionally quite 'blue-collar'.

I grew up Catholic and I went to a Catholic school. Especially in the 80s and 90s, there wasn't much progressivism in my Catholic community – in fact, quite the opposite. You would go to hell for masturbating, so masturbating over a female would be twice as bad!

I went to a Catholic girls' school, so there was lots of 'I bet that teacher is a lez' – you know that sort of negativity. Lesbians were seen as gross. Those comments weren't necessarily directed squarely at me. I was a funny girl in high school: I cracked jokes, I was the class clown, which I think is a classic gay self-preservation manoeuvre.

When I was going through puberty, I had a kind of sexualized dream about a woman that I knew and so I told my mum pretty urgently because I was weirded out. My mum is so lovely. She just calmed me down. She said, 'Look, you're going through puberty right now, so you're going to think all sorts of weird things. Don't bother thinking about this for another second.' I don't think she meant it in a negative way. She was just trying to make me feel better. So, I thought, 'I'm going through puberty. Just because I'm fantasizing about women doesn't mean I'm gay! It's just that my hormones are going bonkers and eventually they'll settle on men.' That was my logic. I genuinely didn't think I was gay.

I finally admitted it to myself when I was in university. I went to university in New York City, which is a great playground for a gay kid coming out. But boy, did homosexuality need to really work hard with me, because I stayed in the closet for three of my four years of university! I even had a gay best friend! There I was, in the most bountiful place on earth for being a young lesbian, and I did nothing about it.

I finally came out in the summer between my third and my final year. I went and saw the movie *Bound* with Gina Gershon and Jennifer Tilly. I watched that and then I had several fever dreams after that.

And then the first person I actually came out to, besides myself, was a priest!

So, growing up Catholic, I was still trying to live who I was in New York City. I didn't want to go to New York City and become a completely different person. So, I was still going to church every Sunday morning. It was in a very progressive neighbourhood, so this was not a very 'fire and brimstone' brand of Catholicism. This was a nicer, sort of reformed, liberal branch of Catholicism. And it was a church in Chelsea, which historically is a pretty gay neighbourhood in New York City. I went to a confessional and the priest is behind the thing, and I just say, 'I think, I think I might be gay.'

Now, technically they're not really allowed to be like, 'Cool!' Regardless of their own feelings, they've got to give what the Pope prescribes as how to deal with these situations. So, I am quite fearful at this point, really expecting that the priest is going to tell me that my soul needs to be cleansed, and that I need to do this, that and the other thing. But instead – and I really thank god that I was at this point in my life in a church in Chelsea in New York City – he said, 'Well, okay. Alright. Well, I'm supposed to say some things, but let's just talk a little bit more about this. Have you acted on your gay feelings?' And I said, 'Well, no.' Because I hadn't.

He said, 'Okay, well what I'm going to say to you technically isn't the line that I'm supposed to use but I would say in your gay relationships treat your partners like I would ask you to if you were straight.' Basically, I think his advice was just don't go out and be a gay hooker! If you're going to fall in love with someone, respect them and respect yourself. So, he sort of gave me a very cautious 'It's okay.' Basically, just be a good gay Catholic in your relationships. And that's exactly what I needed to hear. I think people's experiences with religion vary greatly depending on where they are in the world. I think geographically I was just very lucky. It was a massive relief to feel and understand that I'm not crazy. There are people in the world, even in religion, that don't think I'm going to burn in hell for just basically living my truth. Then it made me consider, 'Who am I going to tell next?'

It took me like a few days to think about it: 'How do I want to talk about this? What's the order of people I'm going to tell?' My best friend was next.

I was watching *Bound* (again!) with him and his boyfriend and there is a line in the movie where Joe Pantoliano says, 'You fucking queers, you make me sick!' So, I looked over at them and said the line, and they were like, 'Katie!' And I said, 'I'm allowed to say it, I am one.' My friend was very pleased for me. I think he knew. But he also knew you can't force someone out of the closet. So, he was my comfort that summer.

Then I went home and I told my mum and she was a lot better than I thought she would be. My parents are divorced and so I told my dad shortly after my mum. My dad had always been like a liberal hippie kind of thinker, so I guess I was less worried about him, because my mum was the religious one in the family. My dad was very cool. About a week into it, he was like, 'Well, okay, here are some books. I've read *Completely Queer: The Gay and Lesbian Encyclopedia* and Chastity Bono's autobiography.' And I was like, 'Okay, thanks!'

My mum wound up being what I would call a 'good kind of Christian'. I told her at the kitchen table. I sat her down and I asked her the question I think that a lot of gay people want to know, which is 'Did you ever think that maybe I might be gay?' I wanted to know what she was thinking about my lack of boyfriends and my lack of expressed sexuality. And she said something like, 'Well, I thought it might be a possibility, but I would never want to vocalize that because I don't know.' I said, 'I wish you could have just asked me!' and she said, 'Well, it's okay.' And then she took me to Pizza Hut so that I could have a good cry over some pizza.

My mum's a good mum. She's always been a good support to both me and my sister. You know, it wasn't about her, it was about me, so she never took the position of 'What did I do?' or 'Where did this come from?'

I wonder whether if she had asked me when I was growing up, that might have pushed me further into the closet. I wasn't ready before I was 20. You can't rush these things. If I had gone to a different university, like something more rural or a smaller town, I probably would have stayed in the closet even longer.

I do have a happy ending to my story. I was doing stand-up in New York City and my wife was sort of living there, very temporarily, and saw me. She bought me a beer and I'm just really bad at one-night stands, you know. So, 18 years later…!

Whenever I do stand-up, I say, 'Look, I always come out with one or two jokes that acknowledge that I'm gay.' And it's not necessarily because that's my chosen topic that I want to harp on about, but if I didn't, you as an audience would be distracted. Because I feel like I look gay and if I don't confirm it, you're going to be like, 'Ah, I'm pretty sure she's gay!' So, I'm always coming out. I think that is something that gay people do every time they move into either a new circle of friends or a new workplace.

You don't get to come out once, you come out as many times as you meet a new person.

I would say, 'Don't let anyone push you to come out.' But now I'm on the other side of it, I would also say, 'Go for it!' If things do not go according to plan, take advantage of the hundreds of support network groups. There are people out there that will help you through it and hold your hand and be your friend.

And if you're not sure you're a lesbian? Go and rent *Bound*[1] on DVD or watch *Gentleman Jack*.[2] Watch both, do yourself a favour, have a little marathon!

---

1    *Bound* is a 1996 film starring Gina Gershon and Jennifer Tilly about two lesbians caught up with the mafia.
2    *Gentleman Jack* is an eight-part BBC and HBO television drama broadcast in 2019. Starring Suranne Jones, it is based on the diaries of Anne Lister, who documented her lesbian relationships in Yorkshire in the 1800s.

'As someone who came out three times to my family, I appear to have had more experience than most people I know, and I think in hindsight what's obvious is you never know what people's reactions are going to be, no matter how much you plan. Did my mum expect me to come out as trans in the year 2000? No, she did not. Did I expect her reaction to me coming out to be "But we just had a conservatory built?" Again, no. It seemed like such a big deal at the time because no one else knew; but once they did, it freed up loads of time to worry about other things. And the truth is, once I told people who I was, their struggles with it weren't my problem. To be fair to the few who did struggle... well, they were just finding out something I'd had years to struggle with.'

**Bethany Black**, actor and comedian

# Carl

**'I could have denied it, but it was time for me to be who I really am.'**

*From being dismissed from the Air Force for his 'incompatible homo-sexuality' to becoming Lord Mayor of his home city!*

I guess I really knew I was gay – well, I knew I was different – from the age of seven. I never really felt attracted to girls but I did feel attracted to the lads that were in my classes growing up. I'd try to speak to my mum and she just said it was a phase I was going through; you know, all boys go through this. So, I just assumed it was part and parcel of a phase of life I was in.

Then as school continued and I was about 14 or 15, I was engaging in sexual acts with people at school and also having strong emotions, so I knew I was different. No one ever spoke about being gay and no one educated you about sexuality at school. I remember our sex education class was a cucumber with a condom, and that was basically it! There was no conversation.

When I was around 16, the whole HIV/AIDS epidemic was hitting our TV screens and I remember being absolutely beside myself, seeing these images and thinking, 'I'm going to die of this disease.' It made me think I didn't want to be gay. I remember again speaking to my mum, and again her telling me it was a phase I was going through. She also told me never to tell my dad. He had strong views – bigoted views.

I ended up trying to see a girl. I went through the motions for a number of years and then I joined the Air Force. I'd always wanted to be a firefighter, but you had to be 21 at the time. I went over to Cyprus to see my brother who was in the RAF and I realized they had a fire service. I thought, I really want to get involved, so I applied when I was 17. At the time it was illegal to be in the forces as an openly gay man. It was actually *illegal*. I remember my mum saying, 'But you can't.' I was like, 'Why?' She said, 'Because you told me that you're gay.' And I said, 'But Mum, you've always told me it's a phase I'm going through!'

I loved the Air Force, but I was definitely leading a double, if not triple, life. Being a fireman in the Air Force was quite a macho image. There had been a couple of rumours about me and so I then started seeing this girl but would still see lads whenever I went back home. Then she fell pregnant. We got engaged, but she had a miscarriage and I realized then that I didn't really feel happy with her and I was going along with this relationship just to do what society said was right.

I just wanted my family to appreciate or value who I was as a person.

I was so confused about my sexuality. When I came home on leave I did seek out men. There were no dating apps back then and I couldn't go to the gay bars in case anyone knew I was in the Air Force, so I ended up going through a bit of cottaging and cruising. It was the only way that people could express themselves at that time. It had to be kept a secret because it was illegal and you would get kicked out of the Air Force and go to military prison for at least six months. So, I took a lot of risks.

I was stationed in Ascension Island and I did see a lad for a while and a lot of rumours started. I was petrified. It was about love and it was about emotions rather than just a sexual encounter. So, I threw myself into a relationship with a girl as if it was the best thing in the world to try and cover up a secret.

When I eventually came back from Ascension Island to England, I was off for about a month afterwards and thought, 'What the heck am I doing?' It was a case of needing to be myself. I needed to accept who I am. I had just got a promotion and also the Queen's Commendation and other awards, but I thought, 'No, I need to come out properly, to be myself.' I told my mum again. Again, she said, 'It's a phase you're going through.'

So, then I told my brothers. One of my brothers was fine, but the one who was in the Air Force was the complete opposite. He said, 'You can't tell anyone that I know because if I know that you're gay and you're still in the Air Force and I'm in the Air Force, I would have to report you!' And that's my own brother telling me that. That hurt. That did hurt.

Then I decided that I had to tell my dad. My mum was adamant: 'Don't tell Dad!' But I did, and it was one of the very first times that I remember for many, many years that he gave me a hug and told me that he loved me. He said, 'Look, son, no one ever told me how to live my life, but just be careful and just be safe.' And that was that.

It made me think, 'What if I had come out earlier?' But I look at what I achieved in the Air Force. I loved the Air Force. I still love the Air Force and I couldn't have achieved any of that being out and gay.

After telling my family, I started to go out more and I loved it. I started a relationship too. I had told a couple of people in the Air Force I was gay and they were fine with it. I did get a couple of strange questions though! One lad said, 'I don't get what you do?

When I am at home at the weekend with my girlfriend, I cuddle up on the couch and watch TV. What do you do?' and I said, 'Exactly the same!'

I think the majority of the people at that time didn't know any gay people. We didn't have role-models on TV. The only people we saw were Larry Grayson and Julian Clary, who were both very camp.

Ultimately, there wasn't a happy ending to my Air Force career. The lad I had started seeing wanted us to spend more time together, so he actually phoned the Air Force and told them that I was gay! Then he told me what he had done. I got called in to Officer Commanding headquarters and there were three senior officers there. They just sat me down and said, 'We need to ask you, do you have homosexual tendencies?' And at that minute I could have quite easily said no, and I firmly believe that that would have been that. (I won a lot of awards in the Air Force. I also did a lot of charity work.) But in that split second in my head, I thought, 'It's now that I have to be myself and be honest and true.' I literally just burst into tears and confirmed that yes, I was gay. It was illegal at the time. They could have quite easily put me into military prison for six months. However, they suspended me for six months and sent me back home, because at that particular time, the case brought by Stonewall to overturn the ban of LGBTQ+ people in the military hadn't yet been won.

I worked here and there, and then applied for The Greater Manchester Fire Service. Now the strange thing with that is, even though there's gay people in the Fire Service, it wasn't talked about. I was the first openly gay person to join the Fire Service. Back in 1998 they didn't have any diversity or equality understanding and I was asked on the very first day not to make my sexuality known. I managed that for about two weeks and then I just felt like I couldn't join in conversations about what we had done at the weekend. So, I ended up telling the lads on the course and they were all fine with it and we used to have a lot of banter. But the officers just didn't know how to handle something that wasn't in their normal surroundings. I managed working in the Fire Service for about 18 months and I just didn't like it. I just really didn't fit. So, in 1999, I left.

At the same time, I saw a competition called 'Mr Gay UK'. It's a sort of a beauty pageant contest, and previously the people that had been in it had good bodies but not necessarily great things 'up there'. I thought, 'Where are the normal gays? Where are the role-models?' So, I went for it and I came second for 'Mr Gay UK' in 1999. I looked into it more and realized there was no representation from normal gay people. When you look at places like Manchester, Brighton, Birmingham and London, we had a gay scene. But where were the people to represent those over in Worksop or Derby or Sheffield? I felt really passionate about the fact that they needed representation. So, then I really went for the competition again. I went to different Pride events. I went around speaking to people and asked what they wanted or who was representing the gay community for them. You know, I didn't have the best body, but I could speak to people and I felt passionate about the need for representation. I felt that I could actually represent the community in a different way, and obviously the public thought the same as I went on to win in 2001. I had over 60 per cent of the votes and my family came to see me win, which was great! Even the brother who had told me not to tell anyone I was gay came along. We had come such a long way in those few years, I felt immensely proud, particularly because it wasn't about the beauty pageant side of it all, but because I was going out and speaking to people and becoming an advocate.

Getting kicked out of the Air Force gave me my passion and my strength to become an advocate and represent our community. So, in 2005 I got into politics and became a councillor and realized that there had never been an openly gay Lord Mayor of Manchester. So, I put myself forward. I narrowly didn't win the first year but in 2016 I put myself forward again and won. I'll be honest, I think some people voted for me to see me fail, but I literally went out there and it was about representing the LGBTQ+ community. I wanted to be seen at everything, to *represent*.

I think one of the things that was great over that period as Lord Mayor was that it was all about equality, diversity and inclusion. Being able to go and speak in schools and businesses, being invited to so many different things where the conversation would never have come up. Even going to mosques. I remember breaking the fast for Ramadan and *The Guardian* running a full story about Manchester's first openly gay Lord Mayor being welcomed by the Imam. It just broke down so many barriers. I managed to get some special pink robes made and I led the Manchester Pride parade as Lord Mayor in pink robes! I just think that goes to show that anybody can do anything that they aspire to do.

And thinking about coming out to friends or family... You've got to know when to do it and not feel pressured into coming out. Don't feel that you have to do it because you're being bullied into it. You'll know when the time is right. And speak to the right people. There's a lot of people out there. There's a lot of organizations that you can talk to. You're not alone.

'It's not a race. It's your life and your decision. So, take your time. Once you are comfortable, it is the right time, not before. You don't owe anyone an explanation or justification for being you. It's your life, so live it your way.'

**Divina De Campo**, UK drag queen and runner-up in the first *RuPaul's Drag Race UK*

# Alfie

**'I had to get drunk to tell my girlfriend I was trans.'**

*Alfie shares his experiences of telling his girlfriend, his friends and his family that he is trans and talks honesty about the physical and mental aspects of his transition.*

I think my identity has been developing over time. Some days I'm quite sure of things, and other days I'm not quite so sure of things. So, I'd say I'm very fluid with my gender identity.

It was a really slow process for me to begin with, not something that I realized straightaway. I'm not one of these people that knew when they were really small. I remember when I was in school I wanted to be a teacher but whenever I pictured it, I was always wearing suits. It wasn't something that I really understood. I knew trans men existed but I didn't know any more than that. I think I watched a documentary and that made me realize who I was and helped a lot of things to make sense.

It wasn't until I was about 17 or 18 that I was like, 'Okay, I'm trans!' As soon as I realized this, it was a really fast process for me. I knew exactly what I wanted. The first thing I needed to do was to tell people they needed to call me by a different name and use different pronouns. Luckily, most people around me were quite understanding. I had some good friends at the time.

I told my partner as well, and she was amazing about it. She's really great! I guess I had an advantage as my partner's queer. She isn't straight anyway. But then again, she entered into a relationship with someone who she thought was a certain way and then it turns out they weren't. So, considering all that, she was actually really cool about it. I was really lucky. I couldn't tell her when I was sober though. We were living in a student house at the time and I'd actually gone home for the weekend. I'd been out with some friends and I came back really drunk at like 3 a.m. She was on Facebook at the time, so I messaged her and said, 'I've got something to tell you.' She said, 'It's cool. I kind of guessed something was going on.' I was really scared, but it turned out that I didn't really have a reason to be. We'd only been together for a few weeks, so it was all really new. I was only about 18, so I was still very young and she was still very young as well. I guess that's a lot to deal with if you're not trans yourself and you're quite young and your partner comes out as trans. I guess it's not something you expect to happen!

My family had more of a problem with it. Luckily, having my partner to support me made it easier. I knew that my mum would have a little bit of a problem with it. I'd come out as gay a few years earlier. I'd told her that I liked girls, and she wasn't too happy about that. She eventually said, 'Yeah, okay, let's just get on with it. It's fine.' But I knew there was going to be a bit of an issue with me being trans. When I did tell her, I didn't really know what to say. So, I just said to her, 'What would you say if I said I wanted to be a boy?' I wouldn't phrase it like that now, but obviously I didn't really know what to say. She said, 'You're not. No, you're not!' She just completely dismissed it. She didn't acknowledge that it was really a thing until I went for my chest surgery. So, yeah, it took quite a while! She's there now. We're good now, and she's even referred to me as her son online, which is really nice.

I'm very close to my sister, and she's told me that even when I thought my family were calling me by the right pronouns, they were actually only doing it when I was there; when I was away, they were using my dead name. I remember sometimes my mum would phone me late on a Friday night, when she'd obviously had a few glasses of wine, and she would dead name me then too. I'd correct her straightaway though. She'd try to pass it off like it wasn't a big deal.

I think the term 'dead naming' is becoming more common now amongst trans people, rather than referring to your old name as a 'birth name'. It brings up too many things if people say 'born as'. I think 'dead name' covers it, because the name is dead.

I don't really have a problem talking about the past. I still like to look back and refer to the fact that I was a little girl, for example. I enjoy my history. I'm just a guy with a trans history.

Coming out as trans was different to coming out as a lesbian. At least coming out as trans, I was so sure about it, whereas when I came out as a lesbian there was still something not quite right about it. I knew I fancied girls, so I just assumed I was a lesbian – but that label didn't feel quite right. So, I think that was a bit scarier because I wasn't sure. But when I came out as trans, I thought, 'That's it!' That was actually a lot easier because I knew that's exactly what it was.

Luckily I've got really understanding friends and I surround myself with people who get it. Or if they don't get it, they're really open to learning about it.

The more that I think about it though, I don't really fall into the category of simply 'a man'. It's not 100 per cent that way.

I'm definitely way more masculine-leaning than feminine. I'm definitely not a woman. I'm just not quite 'a man'. That's not to say that trans men aren't men or anything like that. Obviously, if you identify as that, that's absolutely fine. But I just like to put the word 'trans' in front just so people think about my gender before assuming.

I meet hundreds of people every day in work who have absolutely zero idea that I'm trans. I can guarantee that if they met a trans person they'd say, 'Oh you're the first trans person I've ever met!' But they'd be wrong because they'd have met me a few days ago. People meet trans people all the time!

The place where I work now is amazing. It's a really ethical business and it just so happens that everybody there is very open-minded. We have people from all different backgrounds working there – it's really diverse. No one has ever questioned my identity, but they're happy for me to talk about it.

I did have a previous job where I was in a really awkward situation. I had to go for a hysterectomy. I'd heard that if you take testosterone there's a higher chance of getting cancer. It's just a theory, but I didn't want to take that chance. I just thought, 'Well, I'm not going to use my womb, so I might as well have the surgery.' But I couldn't tell my boss what it was exactly because he didn't know that I was trans and I didn't feel comfortable telling him. It was a really uncomfortable experience. I like people knowing that I'm trans because it's part of my identity and it seems weird when people don't know about it.

I'm a musician and a performer now, and I definitely use my trans identity to celebrate my music. Particularly in my stage performance I'm a bit more camp than I normally am and I embrace effeminacy a little bit more. That's because I want to push the boundaries of gender. I'm not particularly like that in real life, but people put characters on when they're on stage, don't they?

My advice to others questioning their gender identity would be to just go with it. Whatever you're thinking or feeling is totally valid and you don't have to fit into any box. I struggled with that a lot. I really wanted to be super-masculine and that's not who I am at all. Well, I do like lifting weights, but that's the only manly thing that I do!

I feel very lucky to be with my partner. I always knew she was a keeper. She was just so cool about me coming out. When I was freaking out about it, she was the one who was really cool-headed. We've been together over seven years and we're now engaged to be married. It will happen at some point, but she wants a really traditional wedding and I want a rustic one in the woods!

I think I'm actually surprised that I'm in the place mentally where we can get married. But when we do get married I don't want that thing where everyone's waiting for the bride to come in. It's my day too, so we're going to come in together. We're going to smash all the traditional gender roles of a wedding!

Since writing their story Alfie has now changed their pronouns to they/them.

# Daisie

'Why do people always think bisexuals want a threesome?!'

*Daisie had no concern about coming out to her family but struggled when her brother was bullied because of her sexuality.*

I think I knew from quite a young age that I was different. Probably at about eight years old, actually. You know when you've got friends over and you play 'house' and you think, 'Oh should we do that? Is that normal?' And then when I was in school in PE, I saw people getting changed and I just thought it was normal that girls just looked at other girls.

But I didn't think I was bisexual. I didn't know what I was. Then I think between 18 and 19 I realized that I *was* actually bisexual. There was something in me that found women attractive as well. Before then, I just thought it was the normal thing to think that other women were attractive. But I didn't know whether I fancied them in that way or if it was just a phase. It wasn't something that I had heard of really, because I'm from such a small village. There are no bisexual people there. There was a gay man, but there were no bisexual women and I don't think there was a single other bisexual person in my school.

The first time I talked about it, I think I was drunk. I was about 18 and I turned around to my friend and said, 'I need to tell you something. I like women. I'm bisexual.' And she said, 'No way! I am too!' and I'm like, 'What?!'

Then I thought, 'Yeah, I'm gonna put it on Facebook!', because I was young and stupid. And then I woke up and deleted it. It was on Facebook for probably about six hours before I deleted it, but it was during the night, so I didn't really get any comments. I thought, 'I can't have that on my Facebook because I've not even told anyone yet, so I can't make it public without telling my parents.'

I told my mum I needed to tell her something. She said, 'Okay, what do you want to tell me?' My mum is so open-minded and so chilled. She's a massive hippie. So, I thought I'm alright to tell my mum. So, I said, 'Mum, I'm bisexual.' And she said, 'Yeah, I know.' I said, 'What do you mean? How?' She said, 'I've always known, I'm your mother. I know everything.'

My dad said, 'That's fine, whatever makes you happy.' But my mum was actually the more excited one, and even said, 'You're never going to get pregnant if you go with women!' (She had been worried about me becoming pregnant at too young an age.)

With my younger brother, it was really tough though. Because there's a nine-year age difference between us, he was still in school. After I told him, he got massively bullied throughout the rest of school because of me being bisexual. Everybody knew everyone's business in my village. My mum told me about the bullying, but my brother just didn't want to speak about it. I just wanted to go down there and tell them off! My mum tried to contact the school, but they were awful. They didn't do anything. I was ashamed of being bisexual then. Knowing that my brother was going through that because of me was horrible. It was horrendous.

He's fine now though. He's so proud of me. I absolutely love him. I worship the ground he walks on.

My older brother didn't speak to me for eight months. He thought it was disgusting. He's the only one in the family that thought that. What seemed to make it worse was that he's a hair stylist. I said, 'Hold on. You are surrounded by LGBTQ+ people! You've got gay friends, men and women. So, why is it so disgusting for your sister to be bisexual?' He couldn't answer that. Since then, we've not had the same relationship. It's been a decade.

I appeared on *The Bi Life*, which was the UK's first bisexual dating show. I'm so glad that a show like that can exist. I had messages from people saying, 'I find it really hard to accept who I am and my parents don't agree with it, but since they've watched the programme with me, they've been more accepting.' It's just really nice. People don't come out, because they are ashamed of who they are. This programme showed that you are okay being who you want to be.

Before the show, the presenter Courtney Act famously said that actually the 'Bs' in the LGBT community numerically make up the biggest proportion and yet you never really hear from them or really see them. And it is hard to be bisexual, because when you say to somebody that you're bisexual, you get all these messages saying, 'Do you want a threesome?' and 'Which one do you prefer?' I've been in a relationship with a guy and he's turned around and said, 'So, are you straight when you're with me?' No, that's not going to change my sexuality! He just didn't understand it. If I'm with someone, I'm with someone. I'm not going to go with the next man or woman, that's not me. But it doesn't change who I am.

On some dating apps, I've seen lesbians put 'No bisexuals!' That makes me feel horrible. It's just awful.

Sometimes it feels like men get paranoid you will run off with a woman, and then some women get paranoid you will run off with a man!

My advice to any bisexual, or someone who isn't sure, would be just be yourself and don't be ashamed of who you are. If you want to explore your sexuality, go for it! Just be honest to yourself and don't be afraid of what other people are going to think.

'The first time I came out, I did it drunkenly. The second time, it was anxiously. The third time, I felt sick to my stomach. Twenty years on, I'm still coming out every day, but the moments hardly register. Now, most of the time, it's as if I'm blinking.'

**Carrie Lyell**, journalist, Editor of *DIVA* magazine

# Richard

**'How can god love me if I'm gay?'**

*For Black British Muslim Richard, realizing he was gay seriously challenged his relationship with both his parents and god.*

I knew I was different from about the age of seven. There was this real feeling that I had attachments to other boys. It wasn't sexual in any way, shape or form but it was an emotional attachment.

I remember seeing a TV show when I was at primary school in which a lad came out to his family. I remember when he said the words, I thought, 'That's what I am.' On the show the word they used was 'homo' and I thought, 'That's me, I'm a homo.' But every instinct told me to keep it quiet. Words like 'queer' and 'bent' were being used in the playground, but my main reason to keep it quiet was I knew it wasn't 'normal'. And I really, really wanted to fit in. I wanted to be a regular kid. More than anything.

I'm a Black guy – both my parents are from the East coast of Africa – and I thought, 'I can't tell anyone I'm gay as I'm already trying to fit in as a Black kid in a school of white kids. I don't want to create any more differences.' Also, my parents raised me to be Muslim and having that faith was such an important part of my life (having to go to mosque every Friday, going to Arabic school, learning the Quran) that the belief I had as a seven-year-old was that I wasn't right with god. I'd heard comments made in the mosque and I knew it wasn't okay to be Muslim and gay. I knew I was a disappointment, not just to my parents, but to my god. I felt that I was letting god down; that I wasn't right and I wasn't normal.

As a Muslim I can draw incredible strength from my faith but I didn't feel strong back then. I felt so terribly confused and very conflicted. I was kind of hoping it would go away. Going to sixth form college changed that. You're allowed to be different. So, I was kind of hanging out with the goths and the emos and the rockers and they stood out, in terms of different hair colour and breaking the rules, wearing their clothes differently, and I was really drawn towards that. Because I thought, you know, instead of trying to be accepted, perhaps it's okay to be different and to stand out a bit more. And they accepted me. A lot of bands they loved had people who presented as queer in some way. David Bowie was openly bisexual and in Judas Priest the lead singer was gay.

So, I came out to a couple of mates and they were great – some thought it was quite cool. But I did lose a lot of friends too. This was a time when being gay was associated with AIDS and a lot of friends thought it was disgusting and never wanted to speak to me again. I was so lucky because two of my teachers, one who was gay and one who was trans, supported me massively. They were a huge inspiration. I saw them living authentic lives.

I knew I had to be true to myself, to be honest, so I told my parents. It was appalling. It was really awful at first. It was heartbreaking for my mum, and she was tearful for such a long time because she didn't know what it meant. My dad reacted by telling me he could take me to the doctor's because the doctor had tablets that could make me better and cure me of my gayness. So, that was an interesting conversation! But, what was great was I knew at a very deep level that there were no tablets, and at that point in my life I actually felt older than my dad in terms of wisdom. I told him, 'Dad, there aren't any tablets that can stop me being gay.' He conceded, and then he sat me down and told me that through his trade union (because he worked as a shop steward) he'd actually fought for some of the freedoms of the gay employees in his workplace. He'd never really spoken about it and he said that whilst he accepted gay people in his workplace, he couldn't accept that his son was gay as it was too close to home, it was too uncomfortable. And that made me really angry. I thought, 'Hang on a minute, you can befriend people in work and be okay with them but you can't befriend me and I'm your son.' I didn't understand what it meant for me.

I knew what they were thinking: they were wondering how this fitted in with their faith. They didn't want to know if any of my friends were gay, just that they were my friends. They obviously didn't want to know if I had a boyfriend. That upset me enormously. I wanted my parents to see me for who I was and not for who I was pretending to be. Because I pretended for such a long time. It's been a really long journey for them. It took them years. It was a big learning curve for them.

Today? My parents are supportive of gay causes, they support gay marriage and equality. I've been able to reconcile my faith with my sexual and emotional identity. I'm able to still have a faith and be a gay man. I got so much help from amazing organizations. I'm out to everybody now. I don't feel the need to hide anymore. I want to be an out role-model for other queer people. Queer people, especially those teachers, really helped me. Now it's my turn to give back. I helped to set up an LGBTQ+ young people's service in Manchester, where they are supported to feel good about who they are. It consists of groups and counselling support and is around to this day. The service also supports young people in schools and colleges.

My advice for others coming out is to know that however you feel right now, one day you will feel happiness and joy about who you are. Just give it time – an extra day, month or year – because your life *will* improve.

# Louise

'She told me it was illegal to be
a lesbian!'

Credit: Sheralee Lockhart

*Poet, playwright and performer Louise
Wallwein MBE, came out to a social worker, whilst being raised by
nuns in a care home.*

I would say I was really, really young when I started to get
crushes on women, but I don't think I had a word for it. The
first time I heard the word 'lesbian', I remember it was an insult
against somebody else and for a while I thought I didn't want
to be one of them. The way the insult was used kind of sounded
like a disease.

When those feelings got stronger, at secondary school, it was
something I hid even more. I certainly didn't want to be called a
lesbian. But I definitely knew I was one. I blame Martina Navratilova, you know. The minute that started to happen, I knew I
had my hero and I just thought, 'Yeah, I'm a dyke.' But I didn't tell
anyone for a bit, because I was being raised by nuns, and also I
went to a Catholic school – homosexuality was not something
we ever discussed and you only heard about it used as an insult.

I was in care from the age of nine, in many different children's homes. I was in around 13 of them and most of those were run by Catholic nuns. I was being fundamentally educated, not just about homosexuality but also being taught that abortion was evil. Because I was a child that was given away at birth they often talked to me about how lucky I was that I was Catholic and that my mother didn't believe in abortion. So, I owed my existence to Catholicism... And actually, I really was quite moral as a kid.

The final children's home that I was in was for young women and we had a lot more independence. However, it was run by a woman who reacted really badly when I came out to her. She would often threaten to send for the police if I went to a gay club. She kept trying to convince me that it was illegal to be a lesbian! I had started to hang out with activists, though, and learn about human rights. I knew the story that Queen Victoria apparently didn't recognize the existence of lesbians and that's why there was never anything in law about us. But this woman was a fundamentalist Catholic and was running a children's home. Because I don't wear makeup or dresses, she reported that I had hygiene issues. She was always trying to get me to 'woman up'. I got access to my files last year and they are full of comments about my boyishness and about how that's a behavioural problem. So, I was up against it.

I managed to get myself out of care six months early because they just couldn't contain me anymore. I'd already been to Greenham Common and I'd become a full-on activist. I got my first flat by going to the housing office in Manchester and claiming political asylum. At the time, Manchester was like this revolutionary council that was doing all these amazing things and funding LGBT projects. I told them what the woman running the care home was doing and saying, and I got my flat. Looking back, I was much too young at 17. I didn't know how to manage a home. Most weeks I didn't eat, but the woman at the care home was making my life so hard, I had to leave.

My social worker was great. In fact, I had a huge crush on her and told her. She was very kind to me and she was the one who encouraged me to get into activism. She nearly lost her job because she supported me and the choices of a gay person whilst working for a Catholic organization.

At the same time, Clause 28' was announced. I was out and staying out, and I became very involved in the fight against Clause 28. One night in a bar I was given a leaflet about banning the promotion of homosexuality in schools and libraries and any council-funded services. Bear in mind I had recently had this heck of a battle just to get a flat and some freedom, so when I read it, it really wound me up. What Clause 28 meant was things like libraries wouldn't be able to have queer literature. Now, before I left care, the only thing that I had was books, and somehow I was able to find books with lesbians in them. So, I was livid that they wanted to take that away from other young people. I didn't really understand the rest of it; I just saw that queer books were going to be banned and I thought, 'Hell to

---

1    Section 28 of the 1988 Local Government Act was brought in by the Conservative government (led by Margaret Thatcher) to prohibit the promotion of homosexuality by local authorities. It stated that councils should not 'intentionally promote homosexuality or publish material with the intention of promoting homosexuality or promote the teaching in any maintained school of the acceptability of homosexuality as a pretended family relationship'. The clause meant in practice that teachers were prohibited from discussing same-sex relationships with students, and council-run libraries were forbidden from stocking literature or films that contained gay or lesbian themes. The clause was repealed across the UK in 2003.

the no!' So, I went to the meeting and then it rapidly grew and I became a full-time activist.

I was really lucky living in Manchester because of what was going on in the council. They gave us an office when we started campaigning against Clause 28. We had a gay centre; we had the growing Gay Village; I couldn't have been more fortunate. What if I had been somewhere else, perhaps a rural place? I always credit those activists for raising my aspirations. They were all these gorgeous people – lesbians and gay men, all older than me. I was the baby. I really looked up to them and learned loads from them. They talked a different language from me. You know, I was working-class and grew up in care. I was pretty clever but I didn't have the same background as these people and they were amazing. (Yet in the campaign commemorations years later, they said that it was me who pushed them on. I used to drive them mad!)

We'd have these meetings at the town hall and then my fellow activists would just want to go to the pub. But I'd be like, 'No, we've got 200 leaflets. We've got to give them out!' Every week I'd go out into the Gay Village and stand up on a table and tell people that now was the time that we'd got to come out, that we'd got to stop living in the shadows because the longer we lived in the shadows, the more we were going to get attacked. I saw the government as bullies, and the only way to deal with bullies is to stand up to them. And because I used to speak like that, I was sent around the country to spread the word and was always going to London for meetings.

The anti-Clause 28 march in Manchester took place on 20 February, 1988. Twenty-five thousand people turned up and at that time it was the biggest political demonstration of any kind that had ever taken place in Manchester. Considering our political history, that's quite significant. And at the time it was the biggest-ever LGBTQ+ queer demonstration in the world. Ian McKellen[2] was there, Peter Tatchell[3] was there, Michael Cashman[4] was there. I got pushed to the front of the march and I led it with them. It was incredible that all these people had come to my city, and we were all terrified! The police we know now were not the police then. The police chief was all for using 16th-century laws to close down the gay bars. He hated us and we weren't very fond of him either.

I was in a little team of lesbians that the gay men called the 'Shock Troops'. We did all kinds of actions. For example, we stopped all the traffic one night in Piccadilly. There's a famous picture of it in the People's History Museum in Manchester. We were constantly being arrested. We once tried to barge into Granada Studios and onto the evening news.

We never got into any serious trouble with the police – it was mostly public order stuff. My belief is, you never get anywhere in political terms without smashing a few windows. It's all very well being well-adjusted and wanting to be at the table, but it's also a necessary part of any fight to take direct action. For example, the whole reason women and working-class people have the vote is because of a lesbian activist standing up over 100 years ago in the Free Trade Hall with her girlfriend, interrupting a Liberal Party rally attended by Winston Churchill. So, that

---

2    Sir Ian McKellen is a BAFTA and Golden Globe award-winning actor who is also known for his LGBTQ+ activism. He came out in 1988, campaigned against Section 28 and co-founded the LGBTQ+ rights group Stonewall.

3    Peter Tatchell is a human rights campaigner who attempted a citizen's arrest of Zimbabwean President Robert Mugabe in 1999 and again in 2001. He campaigned for LGBTQ+ rights in the 80s and 90s with the group OutRage! and is now the director of the Peter Tatchell Foundation.

4    Michael Cashman is an actor, politician and activist. He played the character Colin Russell in the BBC soap opera *EastEnders* and took part in the first gay kiss in a UK soap. He went on to be one of the founders of the LGBTQ+ rights group Stonewall and then represented the West Midlands as an MEP from 1999 to 2014.

was Annie Kenney and Christabel Pankhurst. Annie was the working-class suffragette, Christabel was part of the Pankhurst family, of course. They were lesbians. That was the moment when women stopped just writing letters (because their letters were being ignored) and started putting the windows out. However, I know my history as an activist and I knew that there was a point at which it was important for the queer movement to sit at the table too.

I've got an MBE[5] now. I was nominated by Arts Council England and it's for outstanding achievement in literature and music and services to the community. Services to the community for me have been my activism. Whatever I have done, I've done it to serve society. I want to improve it and achieve full equality. I felt quite emotional about my MBE and still do. I've felt it profoundly that somebody was asking me if I wanted to be a member of something. I've never had a family. I've never been a member of fuck all. Then I read what it was for and it was amazing. But I was really frightened about the MBE being announced. In the month from when you get the letter to when you accept it, you have to keep it secret. Your mind plays tricks on you and my mind was just telling me, all my mates are going to think I'm a dick!

However, it was amazing. By getting it, I've actually been shown by my community and by my work colleagues and by my friends how much they accept me for who I am and how much they want to celebrate my achievement. I never actually had that before. It made me realize that I've achieved an incredible amount of work. I've talked loads about my activism, but my

---

5    An MBE is one of five classes of appointment to the Order of the British Empire and it rewards contributions to the arts and sciences, work with charitable and welfare organizations, and public service. Candidates must go through a rigorous nomination process and such honours are considered highly prestigious.

actual writing career has been incredible. By accepting the first offer when I was 17 to write a play, by becoming an artist, I was allowed to serve society through the magnetic power of poetry. That's what I do. That's the umbrella for everything.

I'm not going to lie, it's actually been really hard because it's taken 30 years for society to catch up with that very political decision we all took in Manchester in 1988 to say, 'We're coming out and we're staying out!' There is also a difference in experience because of class. The working-class experience took a while longer. It took longer for the estates to fucking catch up. So, you are literally getting your head beaten and kicked in all the time. The thing is, being working-class and actually living in the estates that hadn't been done up yet, I got chased every day for a number of years. I got chased every single day for being gay. The questions would always start with 'Are you a boy or a girl? Are you a man or a woman?' Sometimes I legged it, sometimes I stood my ground. I got my jaw broken twice. I got threatened with rape thousands and thousands of times. You know, 'corrective rape', because they'll show me what a 'real' man can do.

I could never go back in the closet. I would argue that I am a handsome dyke. There are women in the world that are handsome. And you know, we have this weird obsession in our world that men should look one way and women should look another. But the thing is, I was born this way. I still get patted down by male security guards at airports because they think I'm a lad. Thank god for gender neutral toilets as well, as that will save me so much of the abuse that I still face.

For anyone who is questioning their sexuality and is afraid to admit to themselves and to other people that they are part of the LGBTQ+ community, the first thing to say is, 'It's going to be alright.' You are who you are and nothing's going to ever change that. Find your people. I was dead lucky. I found all those activists and I found a cause and that unity. But also, find people that may not be exactly like you, but think you're alright. You can trust them as well. Just remember that unity is our strength and find those people. You can find your local LGBTQ+ centres too. You can find phone numbers online and reach out! If you feel isolated, then call them. They're not just saying 'call this number', they mean it! Don't just hang out with other queer people either. Go and inhabit all the spaces of your city or your town. You have a right to be there. You can have your Gay Village or your pubs and all of that, but you also have a right to own the whole of the city.

'The closet is a weird fishbowl which distorts and distances the world around you. Only by coming out do we start to experience life, love and friendship properly. Reactions can vary – my mother was not happy for a year but ended up driving a Pride float. Be brave: there's a world of love waiting.'

**Jonathan Mayor**, comedian

# Glossary[1]

Please note that this is not a definitive list. These are the latest definitions at the time of going to press. We are aware that terminology is ever-changing and evolving. People are at liberty to define themselves in any way they're comfortable with.

**BAME**: Abbreviation of the term Black, Asian and Minority Ethnic.

**Biphobia**: Prejudice and discrimination towards, fear, and/or dislike of someone who is bisexual or who is perceived to be bisexual, based on their sexual orientation.

**Bisexual/Bi**: Someone who is attracted to people of the same gender and other genders.

**Cis-gender/Cis**: Someone who identifies with the gender they were assigned at birth; someone who is not transgender.

---

1    Adapted from material kindly provided by LGBT Foundation www.lgbt.foundation

**Coming out**: The disclosure of one's LGBTQ+ identity to someone else. Coming out is rarely a once-in-a-lifetime event as many LGBTQ+ people may want or need to come out to each new person they meet or may realize different facets of their LGBTQ+ identity over time which they might then choose to disclose.

**Conversion Therapy**: Activities and therapies that are performed on LGBT people in an attempt to change their sexual orientation or gender identity to that which conforms to a cis- and heteronormative view of society.

**Deadname**: The birth name, or other former name, of someone who has changed it. To deadname someone is to refer to them by their birth name without their consent and is commonly attributed to trans and/or non-binary people who have changed name as part of their transition.

**Equality Act (2010)**: In the UK, this refers to the Equality Act 2010, which provides people with protection from discrimination and ill-treatment based on sexual orientation, gender, gender reassignment and 6 other protected characteristics.

**Gay**: Someone who is almost exclusively romantically, emotionally or sexually attracted to people of the same gender. The term can be used to describe anyone regardless of gender identity but is more commonly used to describe men.

**GB**: The abbreviation of gay and bisexual.

**GBT**: The abbreviation of gay, bisexual and trans.

**Gender**: The socially constructed and reinforced divisions between certain groups (genders) in a culture including social norms that people in these different groups are expected to adhere to, and a person's sense of self relating to these divisions

**Gender Assigned at Birth**: The gender that a person is assumed to be at birth, usually based on the sex assigned at birth.

**Gender Fluid**: Someone whose gender is not fixed; their gender may change slowly or quickly over time and can switch between any number of gender identities and expressions, as each gender fluid person's experience of their fluidity is unique to them.

**Gender Identity**: A person's internal feelings and convictions about their gender. This can be the same or different to the gender they were assigned at birth.

**Gender Neutral**: Something that has no limitations to use that are based on the gender of the user.

**Genderqueer**: Someone whose gender is outside or in opposition to the gender binary. Often viewed as a more intentionally political gender identity than some other non-binary genders, through the inclusion of the politicized 'queer'.

**Gender Reassignment**: The protected characteristic which trans people are described as having, or protected characteristic group they are described as being part of, with reference to the Equality Act 2010. A person has the protected characteristic of gender reassignment if the person is proposing to undergo, is undergoing or has undergone a process (or part of a process) for the purpose of reassigning the person's sex by changing physiological or other attributes of sex.

**Heterosexual**: Someone who is romantically or sexually attracted to someone of a different gender, typically a man who is attracted to women or a woman who is attracted to men.

**HIV/AIDS**: Stands for Human Immunodeficiency Virus / Acquired Immune Deficiency Syndrome. HIV is an STI that attacks the immune system. It is not curable but is treatable and someone with HIV can now be expected to have a normal life expectancy and not be able to transmit the virus while taking medication correctly. It is usually associated with MSM but also has higher than normal prevalence in Black, Asian, and Minority Ethnic communities. HIV progresses to AIDS without treatment. While the person will not die of AIDS itself, the compromised immune system as a result of AIDS means the body is susceptible to infection and unable to fight it, leading to death.

**Homophobia/Homophobic**: Prejudice and discrimination towards, fear, and/or dislike of someone who is, or who is perceived to be attracted to people of the same gender as themselves, based on their sexual orientation.

**Homosexual**: A term used to describe someone who is almost exclusively attracted to people of the same gender. Some consider this word too medical and prefer the terms 'gay', 'lesbian or 'queer'.

**Internalized homophobia**: The feeling of self-hatred experienced by LGBTQ+ people. Often the result of hearing and seeing negative depictions of LGBTQ+ people. It can lead to low self-esteem and other mental health problems.

**Intersex**: A person whose biological sex characteristics, don't fit into the binary medical model of male and female. This can be due to differences in primary and secondary sex characteristics including external and internal genitalia, hormones, and/or chromosomes.

**LB**: The abbreviation of lesbian and bisexual.

**LBT**: The abbreviation of lesbian, bisexual and trans.

**Lesbian**: A woman who is largely or exclusively emotionally, sexually, and/or physically attracted to other women.

**LG**: The abbreviation of lesbian and gay.

**LGB**: The abbreviation of lesbian, gay and bisexual.

**LGBT**: The abbreviation of lesbian, gay, bisexual and trans.

**LGBTphobia/LGBTphobic**: Prejudice and discrimination towards, fear, and/or dislike of someone who is LGBT or who is perceived to be LGBT, that is based on their LGBT identity.

**LGBTQ+**: The acronym for lesbian, gay, bisexual, transgender and queer (sometimes also used to refer to questioning, usually when working with younger age groups). There are variations on this that include more (or fewer) identities, such as LGBT or LGB. LGBTQ+ can also be used to be more inclusive of other identities beyond those described by the acronym but related to them in identity or experience.

**Minority Stress**: Minority stress describes chronically high levels of stress faced by members of stigmatized minority groups.

It may be caused by a number of factors, including poor social support and low socioeconomic status, but the most well understood causes of minority stress are interpersonal prejudice and discrimination.

**Misgender**: The act of referring to someone as the wrong gender or using the wrong pronouns (he, she, boy, sister, etc.). This usually refers to intentionally or maliciously referring to a trans person incorrectly, but of course can also be done accidentally.

**MSM**: Stands for men who have sex with men/men loving men. Men who have sex with men is used as a term within sexual health and other services to make these services more inclusive to men who have sex with other men but may not identify as LGBTQ+.

**Non-binary**: Used to describe those whose gender does not fit into the gender binary. The term can be used by some as an identity in itself and is also used as an overarching term for genders that don't fit into the gender binary, such as genderqueer, bigender and gender fluid.

**Outing/Out**: Disclosing someone else's sexual orientation or gender identity without their consent.

**Pansexual/Pan**: Someone who is emotionally, sexually, and/or physically attracted to others regardless of gender identity.

**Pride**: Having a positive view of membership of the LGBTQ+ community. Also, a celebration of LGBTQ+ cultures, protest at discrimination currently faced, and a reminder of past crimes and discrimination against the community.

**Protected Characteristic**: Under the Equality Act 2010 It is against the law to discriminate against someone because they have a protected characteristic. These are outlined under the act, and comprise: age, disability, gender reassignment, marriage and civil partnership, pregnancy and maternity, race, religion or belief, sex, sexual orientation.

**Queer**: An overarching or umbrella term used by some to describe members of the LGBTQ+ community. The term has been reclaimed by members of the community from previous derogatory use, and some members of the community may not wish to use it due to this history. When Q is seen at the end of LGBTQ+, it typically refers to queer and, less often, questioning.

**Sex:** The scientific and/or legal classification of a person as male, female or intersex. A person's sex is usually determined by a combination of primary and secondary sex characteristics including chromosomes, hormones, and internal and external reproductive organs.

**Sexual Attraction**: Desiring sexual contact with a specific other person or group of people.

**Sexuality**: Sexuality is a holistic term for someone's sexual behaviours, attractions, likes, dislikes, kinks, and preferences. Sexual orientation makes up a part of someone's sexuality, and sexuality is sometimes used interchangeably with sexual orientation, but it covers more than just who a person is attracted to. Sexuality is what you enjoy and how you enjoy it, whether that be partners or activities.

**Sexual Orientation**: How a person feels sexually about different genders. The term describes who they are most likely to pursue a sexual relationship with. Sexual activity does not indicate sexual orientation, so people who have sexual relations with someone of the same gender may not necessarily identify as LGBQ+. This is why terms such as MSM are used in some contexts. Sexual orientation is a protected characteristic under the Equality Act 2010.

**Trans**: An umbrella term to refer to anyone whose gender identity doesn't completely match the gender they were given at birth. This includes, but is not limited to, trans women, trans men, and non-binary people.

**Transition/Transitioning**: Transition relates to the process a trans individual undertakes to align themselves with the gender they are, as opposed to that which they have been assigned at birth. Transition includes some or all of the following cultural, legal and medical adjustments; telling one's family, friends and/or co-workers, changing one's name and/or sex on legal documents; hormone therapy and possibly (though not always) some form of surgical gender affirmation. This is a deeply personal process that may involve medical interventions but does not have to.

**Trans Man**: A man who is trans. Somebody whose gender identity is male and who was assigned female at birth.

**Transphobia/Transphobic**: Prejudice and discrimination towards, fear, and/or dislike of someone who is trans or who is perceived to be trans, that is based on their trans identity.

**Transsexual**: An older and medicalized term used to describe someone living as a different gender than the one assigned at birth. This is sometimes used exclusively to describe trans people who have medically transitioned i.e. undergone hormone replacement therapy and/or gender affirmation surgery. The term is still used by some transgender people but has widely been replaced by trans or transgender, as it is nowadays often considered offensive or exclusionary due to its medical and pathologizing context.

**Trans Woman**: A woman who is trans. Somebody whose gender identity is female and who was assigned male at birth.

**WSW**: Stands for women who have sex with women/women loving women. Women who have sex with women is used as a term within sexual health and other services to make these services more inclusive to women who have sex with other women but may not identify as LGBTQ+.

# Resources

**LGBTQ+ Support and Advice**

The following organizations and charities can provide information and support for you and your families. Please note there are many local LGBTQ+ charities and organizations, and you can find community services in your local area via the following Stonewall link: https://www.stonewall.org.uk/help-advice/whats-my-area

**akt (formally the Albert Kennedy Trust)**
https://www.akt.org.uk
A nationwide LGBTQ+ homelessness charity providing advocacy and training in addition to housing.

**Allsorts**
https://www.allsortsyouth.org.uk
A Brighton-based organization supporting and empowering young people who are LGBTQ+.

### FFLAG (Families and Friends of Lesbians and Gays)

https://www.fflag.org.uk
A charity supporting parents and their lesbian, gay, bisexual and trans sons and daughters.

### Gendered Intelligence

http://genderedintelligence.co.uk
A nationwide, trans-led charity, delivering trans youth work, school mentoring, art projects, training and policy work.

### Imaan

https://imaanlondon.wordpress.com
The UK's leading LGBTQI Muslim support organization.

### LGBT Foundation

https://lgbt.foundation
A national charity delivering advice, support and information services to lesbian, gay, bisexual and trans (LGBT) communities.

### LGBT Health and Wellbeing

https://www.lgbthealth.org.uk
Offers support and social events for LGBT people, with specific trans and non-binary events, to improve the wellbeing of the community across Scotland.

### LGBT Youth Scotland

https://www.lgbtyouth.org.uk
Scotland's national charity for LGBTQI young people, offering support groups, advocacy and training.

### Mermaids

https://www.mermaidsuk.org.uk
Hosts a support group for parents/carers of young gender variant

people, as well as services and campaigning for those children themselves.

## Mindline Trans+
https://bristolmind.org.uk/help-and-counselling/mindline-transplus
A UK-wide phone service offering mental health and emotional support to gender diverse people who need it.

## MindOut
http://www.mindout.org.uk
A Brighton-based mental health organization serving the LGBTQ+ community.

## National Trans Youth Network
https://www.ntyn.org.uk
Representing all the trans youth groups across the UK.

## PFLAG
https://pflag.org
The first and largest organization for lesbian, gay, bisexual, transgender and queer (LGBTQ+) people, their parents and families, and allies in the USA.

## Sparkle
https://www.sparkle.org.uk
A nationwide group and events-based trans organization.

## Stonewall
https://www.stonewall.org.uk
Campaigns for the equality of lesbian, gay, bi and trans people across Britain.